GO TO THE PEOPLE

Travel with Awareness

Christians Aware

Editors

Barbara Butler
Ailsa Moore

Contents

Our Thanks

Our thanks go first of all to our Christians Aware International Committee. The members have kept a constant interest in this book, have read it twice and offered advice.

Other than ourselves the members of the committee are:

Gordon Couch
Roger Millman
John Moore
Florence Nyahwa
Robert Taylor

Dr. John Moore has written the section on 'Health and Travel'. He is a lecturer and paediatrician who works regularly in Africa. He leads Christians Aware groups in Africa.

Roger Millman has written the sections on 'Going in a Group with Christians Aware' 'Travel Guides' and on the 'Use of information supplied by embassies and national tourist boards'. He is a geographer who was a founding member of "Tourism Concern", is currently on the Christians Aware Council and runs a small personal consultancy in responsive travel.

Gordon Couch has written on 'Going with Disability.' He is the author of "Access in Israel and the Palestinian Authority," and of "Access in London." He leads Christians Aware groups in India.

Zara Fleming has written a reflection on preparing to take a group on pilgrimage to Mount Kailash. She was the chair of the Tibet Society.

Denise Moll, a peace worker and member of the Gandhi Foundation, has written her reflection on her visit to Ladakh

We are grateful to Simon Curl for his artwork which we have used in the title page and on pages – 5, 9, 71, 103 and 131.

We are grateful to all our photographers and other contributors.

The front and back covers and the designs on the title page and page 5 are by Paula Curtis, University of Leicester, AVS-Graphics.

Quotations

'To travel properly you have to ignore external inconveniences and surrender yourself entirely to the experience. You must blend into your surroundings and accept what comes. In this way, you become part of the land, and that is where the reward comes.'
Dame Freya Stark (20th Century traveller and writer)

'The use of travelling is to regulate the imagination by reality and instead of thinking how things may be, to see them as they are.'
Dr. Samuel Johnson (18th Century lexicographer, critic and conversationalist)

'It is one of the disasters of modern life that people, instead of journeying, want to be already at the goal….and yet the journey can be so rich in encounters and so rich in experience….. There is no need to reach the goal as quickly as we can, because what matters is that every step of this journey should have been meaningful and rich in content.'
Most Reverend Metropolitan Anthony of Sourazh (from a conference talk)

'It is better to travel hopefully than to arrive'
Robert Louis Stevenson (from 'Travels with a Donkey')

The key to humanisation of travel is the new, all-round individual. Not just a holiday person, but a human being; aware of him/herself (and of others) and of his/her travel motives and desires: one who has learnt to be self-critical and to use his/her experience of other cultures to see him/herself in a new light. This person will have undertaken, or be prepared to undertake, what we may call an inner journey, on the way to acquiring knowledge, humility and a willingness to share these qualities. Only then will we be able to bring to travel more humanity.'
Jost Krippendorf (from the 'Holiday Makers')

Foreword

Dervla Murphy

Here we have a guidebook with a difference, a guide to humane, intelligent travelling. While offering much sound advice to the novice, "Go to the People" will also help those who have wearied of conventional tours – perhaps in organized tours, perhaps as back-packers – and wish to experience other lands not merely as onlookers/fun-seekers. Holidays abroad have long since been taken over by the 'Leisure Department' of the consumer society. For too many, foreign countries have become items on their lists of possessions – 'I've been to X,Y & Z, and here are the photographs.' This attitude – essentially sterile for the 'consumer' – is countered by "Go to the People." A holiday can be exciting, and its benefits durable, less because of numerous passport stamps from 'exotic' border posts than because the traveller has been privileged to meet individual representatives of unfamiliar cultures and to share, however briefly, in their way of life, not seeing them as 'local colour' but relating to them as other human beings.

Since the introduction of cheap airfares mass tourism has done immense damage, both to the global environment and to numerous hitherto remote regions. In such places, the integrity of local cultures has been shattered by the abrupt intrusion of the least desirable elements in our Western lifestyle. This is undeniable; the argument that 'tourism helps backward economies' was soon demolished by events. True, more cash circulates, allowing people to acquire possessions previously beyond their reach. But that 'benefit' is usually outweighed by a morale-corroding dependence on tourist dollars, leading to a loss of communal self-respect. There follows, in many cases, a tragic distortion of the traditional economy as shoddy, mass-produced goods and processed foods undermine those crafts and skills which for centuries (sometimes millennia) gave satisfaction and status to their individual practitioners.

In times past, those few who could afford to travel had an interest, real or feigned, in art, architecture, antiquities. The average contemporary tourist has no such pretensions yet, if 'packaged', must swallow his/her daily dose of 'culture' and obediently follow the guide through cathedrals, museums, temples, palaces, art galleries, archaeological sites – twenty minutes here, forty five minutes there, thirty minutes somewhere else. Then back on the bus – eyes glazed, film used up – and off to the next dosage point. Nowhere is there an opportunity to make friends with the ordinary people of the country.

As the gap between rich and poor widens, and desperate refugees and asylum seekers seem to threaten the West's complacently affluent societies, the importance of establishing such personal relationships, while seeking to understand other cultures, cannot be overstated. That infamous gap, which has been inexorably widening since globalisation took off, fills some people (though not enough) with despair. We feel helpless and angry – an unwholesome combination. Being aware of the machinations of powerful multinational corporations (aka globalizers), our own impotence frustrates us. Yet we are not entirely helpless, as "Go to the People" points out. 'Aware' travellers have already, in certain areas, put a brake on the tourist industry's juggernaut. We can, for instance, vigorously protest against the cruelty of 'protecting' animals in reservations, allowing their 'protectors' to profit at the expense of local populations exiled from their home territories. The traveller-as-consumer must be impressed and gratified. When she/he makes it plain that the excesses of the tourist industry are unacceptable, the profiteers listen. Like all salespersons they want to please their customers.

For any Westerner seeking to share in the lives of others, some degree of culture shock is at first inevitable. Apart from the comparatively trivial matter of new and sometimes alarming-looking foods, the most obvious test of our adaptability concerns time. Most of us are brought up to value punctuality as a virtue, a component of good manners. And some of us (alas an increasing number) have been conditioned to think 'Time is Money' and automatically to follow that line of thought even when on holiday. We are easily unnerved – made to feel our day is out of control, has been disordered – when A arrives two hours late offering no explanation, or B arrives an hour early and says we must be off at once, or the 8.00.am bus leaves at 11.40am. It is advisable to make the necessary mind-set adjustment as soon as possible, before culture shock hardens into prejudice. When such incidents no longer unnerve or irritate we find ourselves liberated, recognizing that other people's attitudes to time are eminently conducive to the holiday spirit, even if inimical to Western standards of efficiency. (And what, we may legitimately ask, have Western standards of efficiency done for our home planet?)

We have entered an extremely dangerous century, with political leaders of every hue deliberately provoking suspicion, fear and hatred. As their irresponsible, megalomania and manipulation of ordinary citizens' perceptions of the world gain momentum, it is essential, for travellers to go to the people of other countries and feel for themselves our common humanity. Readers of this book will be well equipped to 'travel with awareness' and contribute their mite – which collectively could be a mighty mite – to exposing the globalising bullies and their political henchmen.

Dervla is a well-known traveller and writer. Some of her books are included in our book list.

Seeking to share in the lives of others

Preface

This book is written for every person who plans to travel and for many who have an interest in travelling primarily to meet people, to show interest in their lives and to share their concerns. It is for those who wish to learn about cultures and countries, seeing them, at least in part, through the eyes of those who are part of them. We have written from a Christian perspective and largely, though not exclusively, from the experiences of the Christians Aware international visits and exchanges. We do not however wish for our book to be limited to Christians but rather hope that it will be useful to a much wider readership.

The Christians Aware individual and group visits and exchanges have grown from the primary aim of the organisation: to develop multi-cultural and inter faith understanding and friendship in a spirit of sharing so that a new focus and energy is generated for action towards human development and wholeness.

One important aspect of Christians Aware visits is that the hosts set the agenda rather than the visitors. Travellers are thus enabled to see the places they visit as their hosts see them, rather than to travel in the cocoon of their own culture and expectations. Sometimes, in this way, people are creatively surprised by going somewhere they would never have thought of going, and meeting people they would never have thought of meeting. A British group travelling in Kenya had spent several hours in a mini-bus, and had hoped to see a beautiful hippo pool at the end of the journey. The Kenyan leader disappointed the visitors by announcing that he would like to invite everyone to his grandmother's farm, which would be much more interesting than the hippo pool. The visitors accepted this change in the programme, but with heavy hearts, until they arrived at the farm and were welcomed into a family and community which had been there for hundreds of years. They shared a rare gathering which they would never forget.

Encounter is spiritual. It offers a link between people in their everyday situations and an insight into ordinary life in other cultures which is far from ordinary, but invigorating, enlightening and enabling of life for visitors and hosts alike.

The thrill of being a traveller can be experienced first hand, and through this book we hope to help and inspire 'new travellers' to set off equipped to enjoy and manage whatever comes along.

For those unable to travel or for those not yet ready to undertake the experience, we supply a list of excellent books that can take the reader on unique journeys to lands far and near. Nobody need be deprived of the travel experience whether it is from the comfort of an armchair or on the road itself.

'Bon voyage' to all.

Barbara Butler   Ailsa Moore

Ailsa Moore is a trained biologist and teacher who, more recently, has spent time travelling to a number of areas of conflict where her charity has been working on development and income generating programmes.

Barbara Butler is the Executive Secretary of Christians Aware. She writes and teaches, organises conferences and courses on mission and development issues and travels, mainly to the developing world.

Always try to take half the amount of luggage you think you need

TEN COMMANDMENTS FOR TRAVELLERS

1. Remember if thou wast expected to stay in one place thou wouldst have been created with roots. Travelling can bring joy and enlightenment to the enquiring mind.

2. Thou shalt not expect to find things as thou hast them at home, for thou hast left thy home to find things different.

3. Thou shalt not allow other travellers to get on thy nerves, for thou hast important interests to pursue. Irritation is a distraction.

4. Remember thy passport so thou knowest where it is at all times, for a person without a passport is a person without a country.

5. Remember to take only one half of the clothes thou thinkest thou needest and twice the amount of money.

6. Thou shalt accept gracefully that meeting and encounter are more important than the time at which the meeting happens. Making time a god can become idolatry.

7. Thou shalt not worry. Those who worry have no pleasure. Few things are ever fatal.

8. Thou shalt not make thyself a tourist. When in 'Rome' do somewhat as the 'Romans' do and accept the style of 'Roman' living.

9. Thou shalt not judge the people of a country by the one person with whom thou hast had trouble.

10. Remember thou art a guest in every land, and when thou treateth thy host with respect thou shalt be treated as an honoured guest.

Thinking and Planning

Chapter One

Thinking and Planning

'Two roads diverged in a wood, and I-
I took the one less travelled by,
And that has made all the difference.'
Robert Frost "The road not taken".

Ways to Go

It is vital to think carefully about our journeys, why we want to make them, where we will go and how we will travel. Will we be going on our own, with a group or with family and friends? We may be travelling abroad for the first time and have no contacts in the place we plan to visit, travelling with a friend or in a group may ease our anxiety and apprehension about coping with travel arrangements, passport controls and the many experiences in store.

Going Alone

We may prefer to travel alone or we may have a special reason for doing so. If we travel alone we will certainly have a different experience from the one we would have in going with a friend, our family or in a group. It is possible that the first time we travel alone we may wish to consider a package holiday as a straightforward and simple introduction to a country and its people. This may perhaps be followed by a more creative lone visit to the same place.

When we travel alone we may be very vulnerable and sometimes lonely. Our community becomes the people we meet along the way and at our destination, much more than if we travel with others. If we travel alone we are more likely to learn from a new culture and a new language, because we are free to make the contacts we wish to make and to give our full attention to our friends and hosts, listening and learning without the distractions of travelling companions.

Mark Simpson is someone who travelled alone and who wrote about his experiences when he returned home.

> 'With "A" Levels out of the way, I could begin the task of organising my "year out." As so many people told me, it was an opportunity to do something that I would never do again. I had a desire to spend time in a Third world country where I would be free from Western luxuries. It would be an exciting experience through which I could learn about the important things in life. It would also help me if at any time in the future I was to work overseas.
>
> As I might have expected, the task of finding an organisation to arrange such a thing was difficult. At 18 years old, unskilled and wanting only 6 months experience I was more trouble than I was worth. My plan was to spend the first half of the year working to raise the airfare. Eventually I was put in touch with Christians Aware and things began to look up. There was a chance to go to East Africa, which I liked the sound of. I would be staying with African people, who would give me work to do. I was apprehensive but as it turned out it was much better than I could have imagined.
>
> In February I left home on the cheapest flight possible, and I arrived in Nairobi where I was met and taken in a Land Rover to Murang'a, 100 Km. to the North East,

Going Alone

where I would live for the next few months. On the second day of my visit we made a programme for my stay, including teaching in the Church school for a month, and then moving around to stay with different people and to help them in any way they wished. The teaching arrangement was not possible, and many of the people only wished to help me , and did not wish me to work. Things began to happen after 2 weeks however when I went to stay in St. Nicholas Orphanage in Nakuru for a week. I then went to a remote forestry station high up in the Aberdare Mountains to learn about forestry. An opportunity to teach finally came and I spent the next month living in Thika, the "Birmingham of Kenya" as I once heard it described. I am not cut out to be a teacher but I did introduce some class room games for the younger pupils.

I also had an opportunity to go to Tanzania. I stayed with a friend in Dodoma, to learn what the life of a missionary from overseas was about, and I later helped the school on a three day trip when a male teacher was needed. I also spent some time in Korogwe.

The final few weeks of my time were spent in the desert area north of Mount Kenya at the invitation of a Maasai clergyman. I also went to Mombasa and visited many people around Murang'a. My final week was spent working in a camp in the Maasai Mara Game Reserve.

The trip was a great experience. I learned so much and it was not all great fun. I had times of boredom, homesickness and illness, including malaria, twice. There were times when I was in danger, alone and frightened, especially during the 5-day bus journey to Tanzania. I learnt the necessity of praying. I had the rare opportunity to be as an African in all my journeys and daily living. I had an experience that was ideal for me, and would be good for many people I know. I had an experience that will be invaluable in my life, whether I return to Africa or not.'

Rachel Bull went to Sri Lanka alone just after she had left school, knowing that she hoped to do a degree in Development Studies on her return. She left for Sri Lanka in January 1996 on a six month visit arranged by Christians Aware. She has written about her time in the Woodlands Community Network in the Bandarawela area of the country.

'As soon as I left the airport, all the things I had read about, been told, or seen pictures of in Geography books were there in front of me – cows lazing beside the road with much waggling of heads, three-wheeled taxis- and a bus half full of fridges.

'I was met by Mr. Lloyd Anandapulla and two people from the Woodlands Community. We stayed with Lloyd and his family before travelling to Bandarawela the next day. My first few journeys, or rather my first few modes of transport, (e.g. moped, loose seat held on with wire, no crash helmet, potholes, suitcase balanced on knees) made me realise that however prepared I thought I was, I still had to adjust myself to accept circumstances very unusual to me, something every traveller has had to do.

I worked in the Woodlands Network office, which is also the home of Father Harry Hass. The outside is painted with flowers, and the inside is also brightly coloured, and very friendly. A working day begins at 8.00 a.m. and ends at 4.30 p.m. It is punctuated by two tea beaks. Tea breaks are sacred times in Sri Lanka and even the buses stop at 10.00 a.m. for the driver to have a cup of tea. Lunch is prepared by the Woodlands catering service. The community eats together in the kitchen, a time of lots of laughter. Many things were explained to me about Woodlands Network before I joined them, but it took me several days to come to terms with everything. Because

Go for it

14

Woodlands is a network there are a lot of affiliated groups, and I therefore met a variety of people from many different fields. I learnt about the problems of pesticide use and over-use, and the difficulties and triumphs of growers who want to become organic. I now know a little about the cultural importance and history of some of the island's tourist attractions and about various methods of language teaching. I also discovered, whilst doing group meditation, that I only have control over six of my toes.

One of the places connected with Woodlands Network is Woodlands Farm and Leisure Resort. It is quite as glamorous as it sounds. It is a hostel owned by Christian and Virginia Perera, where long and short term visitors to Bandarawala stay. We had eight such people in our Woodlands family, seven of them German. It was really nice when any of us went to town because we met people we knew, from the market or off the bus, through Woodlands.

I have been faced with some staggering beliefs held by some people about Europe, and I am sure that Sri Lankans in Europe find the same surprising beliefs. This is an area which CA and Woodlands are particularly concerned with, an exchange of knowledge, wisdom and understanding. At Woodlands this mainly means between tourists and local people and happens both through arranged meetings and as chance exchanges. I felt very alive there. I have climbed Adam's Peak at sunrise, and I have also gone on a batik course.'

Mark and Rachel are just two young people who travelled alone and lived in a new culture for the first time. Both of them changed and as Mark said, the experiences will be invaluable for a long time into the future.

Going with Disability

For someone with a disability, there are a lot of additional aspects relating to travelling that need to be considered. A great deal depends on the nature of the disability, and whether the condition is relatively stable, and ultimately, only the traveller can assess whether travelling is worth the extra hassle.

In relation to many things, including cultural and inter-faith understanding, having a disability is no disadvantage. You may well go to places where there is considerably less disability awareness than you are used to at home, and where the facilities you need (or have got used to) just aren't there. Equally, there are some places, generally in some other parts of Europe, and in north America, which can be fascinating places to visit, where you will find that some things are even better than they are at home.

Perhaps the first thing to say is "Don't be put off by potential problems if you really want to travel". I know of someone requiring the use of an 'iron lung' overnight who travelled with two friends overland across Europe, Turkey, Afganistan and Pakistan to India - and this was back in the 1970s ! Not only were they travelling in a somewhat clapped out old car, but the said 'lung' needed a power supply to make it work every night.

While not everyone will want to be remotely that adventurous, our basic comment is that if you really want to go somewhere, then "Go for it !". However, it's very important to be aware of your own level of enthusiasm and interest, of your adaptability, and of the conditions you'll meet en route. Travel certainly broadens the mind, and can give one an insight into people and situations that you just cannot get from reading or from watching the television. The best way to get some kind of understanding of the current situation in Israel, and of the hopes and fears of both Israelis and Palestinians, is to go and meet both groups, and see for yourself what it is like 'on the ground'. Equally, the best way to understand some aspects of Roman or Greek history is to go to some of the great sites around the Mediterranean. The best way to understand Hinduism or Jainism is to go and talk to its adherents in India, and to see and get to understand some of its festivals and its temples and teachings. Disabled people should have this option just as much as others, as far as is humanly possible.

If you go off travelling, even to what people might regard as relatively easy places, you'll almost certainly need a touch of realism and a sense of humour, together with a great deal of both patience and determination. 'Keep smiling' is an appropriate motto, maybe even an extension of the ten travelling commandments, but every now and again, one suspects, you'll probably need to be really determined and forceful.

The most important factors to assess before travelling are:

> Your own needs, about which you must be ruthlessly practical.
> Who you are travelling with (if anyone).
> Your (possible) host/s in the places you're going to.
> Both your adaptability and determination, and that of your possible companions.
> The conditions in the place/s you want to visit, and this includes:
> Your accommodation.
> Method/s of getting around.
> Whether it is in a city, or is mainly rural.
> The distances involved.
> Whether the place is mountainous or flat.
> The climate, and the altitude of the place/s you are intending to visit.
> How much reliable information you can get about the place/s you want to go to;
> whether there are people there who are likely to be helpful, adaptable and knowledgeable about the implications of disability.

An aspect of the whole business of 'travelling with awareness' is an understanding of the fact that many of those from whom you are seeking information, or with whom you are making arrangements and bookings, will not necessarily understand your particular needs. Thus you need to spell out your questions, and make them both clear and precise, so that there is no ambiguity. It is also sensible to explain why you need the information.

For example, it is not enough to ask someone "Is your hotel or hostel accessible?" The answer depends entirely on the other person's perception of accessibility. If, for example, steps are a problem for you, then ask specifically "How many steps are there to get into the hotel, and are there any steps inside in getting to my bedroom and to the dining room". If you have particular requirements relating to the provision of a toilet and/or, for example of a wheelchair accessible shower, then again, ask clear and specific questions, such as "What is the width of the bathroom door? How much space is there alongside the toilet for side transfer from a wheelchair? (You might even e-mail, fax or post a little sketch, showing exactly what you mean) Does the bathroom have a wheel-chair accessible shower, or alternatively, can I put a plastic chair in the shower to make it possible for me to use? You may have to ask "How big is the lift?", and actually get someone to measure it, as in some places, the lift will be too small for a wheelchair.

On the whole it is necessary to discuss things that are important to you directly with the provider - rather than through the filter of a travel agent. Travel agents are well briefed and up to speed in getting people a good deal in terms of cheap flights, and possibly good value accommodation. They are also well briefed about providing information for those wanting arrangements made on a 'business class' budget. In general (and there will obviously be a few exceptions), travel agents are NOT well trained or experienced in providing the specific information that disabled travellers may need - although they may not be willing to admit this.

These days, the web is an increasingly valuable source of information. Do be aware, however, that much of it is poorly researched, and access information in particular virtually always needs following-up and checking. As with most travel guides, access information is poorly researched, and the 'disabled persons' symbol is used without clear criteria as to what it means.

For most people, long distance travel has to be by air, and while the airlines have improved greatly in their attitude to and treatment of disabled people, there are still likely to be a few bumps and bruises along the way. For example, there is no common or agreed policy on the airlines about how (and whether) electric wheelchairs can be carried, nor about how they assess and deal with people with various medical conditions. In the UK there is a very helpful and useful organisation called **Tripscope** (Alexander House, 247 High Street, Brentford, Middx TW8 0NE *Tel:* 08457-585641) which can give advice on all aspects of travelling for disabled people.

If you are travelling to a developing country, then be aware of the implications of the fact that facilities for disabled people may be non-existent. The roads and pavements may be very rough - and traffic conditions chaotic. The only adapted toilets you will find in some countries are the ones at the airport when you arrive. Attitudes to disability will vary widely. In some countries, the only way that some disabled people who live there can survive is by begging. Many disabled people in the world will have no access to modern medical equipment and aids (unless they come from a very rich family), and you may see those who cannot walk for some reason literally having to crawl along the road in order to get around. Such sights can be disturbing.

In many countries, especially if you are visiting for the first time, the first enquiry point may be the local organisations of and for disabled people. The advice and information you get may/will be highly variable, but it may give you a starting point for further enquiries. There is a useful collection of contacts in the *Directory for Disabled People* relating to holidays/travelling.

A few places have *Access Guides*, some of which can be really useful, and, at worst, will provide contacts through whom to make further enquiries. A key question in relation to these guidebooks is 'How was the information gathered ?' Some are based simply on information given by others, thus it is not on a consistent basis – others are based on visits by people applying consistent standards in their investigation, and these are generally of greater value. For examples of well researched access guides, see *Access in London* and *Access in Israel and the Palestinian Authority*, both available from Access Project, 39 Bradley Gardens, West Ealing W13 8HE, UK.

Some years ago, Alison Walsh published a book called *Nothing Ventured* (published by Harrap Columbus, London, 1991) which contained a collection of the tales and experiences of disabled travellers. It also included a great deal of useful advice related to 'planning'. Among other things, she highlighted the highly variable nature of information supplied by Tourism Authorities in different countries. There are a few that can provide quite good information, but most (at best) simply scatter a wheelchair sign through some of their publications without any real attempt to define what that means or to say whether the places have been properly assessed. While the book is almost certainly not still available in bookshops, it should be possible to borrow it through a library.

You may, of course, have specific medical needs when travelling, and, for example, those needing dialysis on a regular basis need to check about the facilities in the place they are visiting. It is

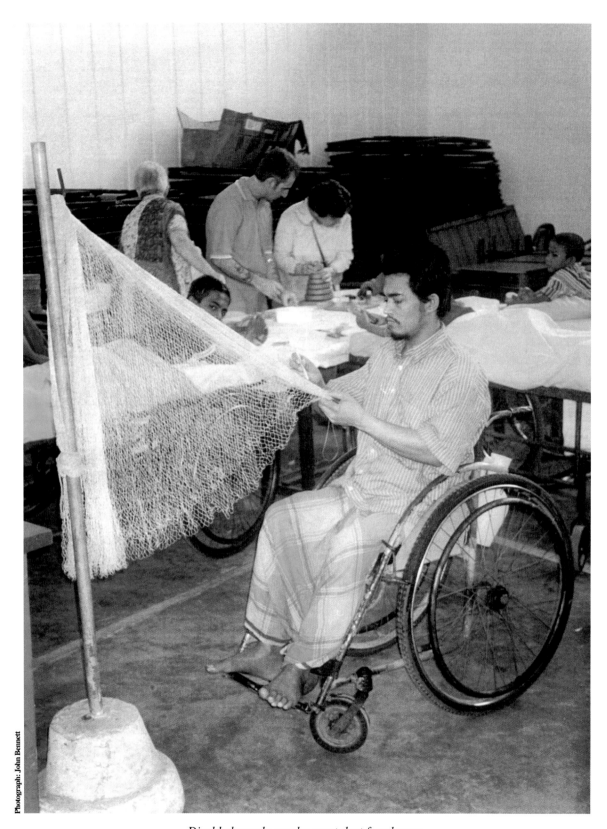

Disabled people can be a catalyst for change

imperative for you to do your homework before setting off, and if there is one general message, apart from 'go for it if you really want to,' it is to 'plan carefully.'

One area to be very careful about is in the travel insurance policy you take out. Do NOT just take the one from your travel agents desk without having a good look at the small print. For up-to-date advice, talk to Holiday Care and RADAR, or possibly the big disability organisations like SCOPE. Standard policies can exclude some claims that might be associated with disability, although, fortunately, there is an increasing awareness that most people won't want to travel if there's an increased chance of them finishing up needing treatment in a foreign hospital miles from home. Most disabled people have stable conditions where the risk isn't any greater abroad than it is at home.

Alongside all the implied warnings discussed above, there are hugely positive aspects of travel. Disabled people can be a catalyst for change simply by getting over the barriers and going to Venice or Reykjavik or Delhi. That is exactly what has happened in the UK over the past few decades. It is the disabled people who have got out and about, and have joined in all the normal things like going to the shops and the cinema, that have forced others to change their outlook (and access provisions). Quite apart from having a huge number of new and exciting experiences, and hence a lot to talk about when they get back, disabled visitors do leave their mark - and that can be a contribution to the long slow process of raising awareness and understanding internationally.

Going with Children

If we are taking children with us on our travels there is a lot we can do to make the whole experience more interesting, certainly more educational and in some ways much easier for us as adults than going without the children. The main thing is to involve the children in the planning, including the discussions about where to go. Even little children can share the plans and perhaps express their opinions. When children are about eight years or older we may prepare a list of possible places to visit and then send the children off to do the research. It would help them to give them an idea of what we need to know, for example, climate, currency, geographical location, culture, past and present history, language, wild-life, religion and so on. The children may be pointed in the direction of the local library or the internet. We must allow plenty of time, and be ready to provide notebooks and maps. We should also set a time for the completion of the work. We may perhaps be surprised at how many skills this research requires, all of which should be helpful in supporting the local school curriculum. We may hopefully be very pleased by the quality of the results. We will then enjoy the review of the work and the making of the collective decision about where to go and why, and what we hope to achieve.

Once we have decided where to go we may begin to plan the actual programme for the visit. Our children will learn from the planning, but will learn incredibly from the venture itself, especially if we have consciously taken the learning possibilities into account. We usually know our children's interests and needs, and may share these in the planning and make sure we cater for them. The main thing to remember is that children need to be kept occupied and interested. They should never be bored, whether at home or on holiday. They also need to know that we need them to be with us. Nothing is more depressing than the feeling that you are not necessary for what is going on, merely a spare part, and easily replaceable by a cardboard cut-out.

Sometimes the children will be better at travelling than the adults and this can be thought through and brought into the planning of a visit. Children make new friends very easily and will delight in meeting local children and being invited into their homes. The children may well, as they do at home, introduce us to new people who may become friends. The children may be encouraged to take

Children enjoy new experiences

along their drawing and painting materials, and to draw and paint throughout the visit, looking and recording carefully. They may also keep a diary and perhaps take the photographs. It is so good for the children to learn to be sensitive towards the needs and feelings of others, and parents and friends can help with this. Children are often less inhibited when it comes to trying out the local language and this can be very helpful at times.

When eleven year old Tamsin went to Uganda in a Christians Aware group she kept a diary. Her entry for one day is:

"Today we went to an end of term school service for the pupils of Luwero Secondary School, which was really nice. After this the adults started painting the vicarage, while Zoe and I taught recorders to 18 pupils, in front of about 30 pupils. We managed to teach them two songs, with no books to give out. We then stopped for a lunch of chapattis, pineapple, saffron cakes, soda and tea or coffee. After lunch all the adults got back to work while Zoe and I taught recorders to a new group of children. After two more hours Dad and I slipped away to buy fruit on a 'border-border.' (motor cycle taxi). We came back with a huge bunch of bananas wedged between me and the driver and the rest of the fruit between Dad and me! When we got back I had to lead Eridard's goat back to him, after filling a jerry can with water at the nearby pump."

No-one could have called Tamsin and her sister 'spare parts' on the visit to Uganda.

We have included some books in our book list which will help in planning visits with children. There are also useful reference books for the children. We especially recommend the books published by the World Wildlife Fund.

Going for Business

Many people who travel do so in the course of their work. It is natural that this group of travellers will wish their travel and the time spent overseas to be as efficiently organized and as comfortable as possible. They may at the same time wish to learn about the culture they are in whilst they do their work and also to share their experiences with others on their return home.

There may also be a little spare time for the business traveller to meet people and to go to places of interest.

"During the past 30 years, intercontinental business travel and tourism has increased at a remarkable rate. Many people think nothing of moving from Rio to Cape Town or from Delhi to Bangkok on business, or visiting the game parks of Zimbabwe, Tanzania and South Africa or the beaches of Goa, Thailand Kenya and The Gambia. In their travels they live in an almost perpetual cocoon, carefully protected from the real lives of the great majority of the people around them. Tourists will stay in high-rise hotels on spectacular sea fronts and will travel by coach out to the mountains and game parks. They may well only be a few blocks from the hotel, but they will not walk there after dark, indeed they will not be encouraged to walk anywhere after dark. They will certainly not see the massive shanty towns that are a feature of so many cities across the world.

The world's elite, numbering many hundreds of millions, is mobile as never before yet travels the world in a perpetual mirage, constantly protected and made comfortable, happily unaware of the real world. Not that such poverty is restricted to the countries of the South. In the last 20 years especially, the rich-poor divide has grown alarmingly in many Northern states, with large districts of many cities just as dangerous as most of Johannesberg, Nairobi or Lagos. Nor is this enduring rich-poor divide restricted to the circumstances of business travellers and tourists – it is demonstrated even more dramatically by the life-styles of the elites."

This extract comes from "Losing Control," by Paul Rogers, by kind permission of the publishers, Pluto Press. It opens our eyes to some of the realities of what is happening in a world where big business is taking control.

Going in a Group

Going in a group is not for everyone but it can be very rewarding to share some of the responsibilities, meet new people and have a leader who is well informed and helpful.

The most creative way for a group to travel is perhaps to meet another group or community. Invitations would normally be initiated by the host community and responded to as a wonderful opportunity offered to visitors to learn from the culture and community they are visiting and to develop friendship. The beauty of the country, or lack of it, should not be relevant in making a decision to undertake such a visit. A group may even accept invitations into suffering situations, to learn from the people there, and to express solidarity with them.

It is vitally important for members of a group to be clear from the outset that group visits are not tourism, and that people who take part in them are not tourists. It is necessary for a leader to be very explicit to potential members of a visiting group about their responsibility not only to be good listeners and learners, but hopefully to be hosts in their turn and to share their experiences with other people, perhaps in their church or community It is possible of course that the impact of a visit takes longer to be realized by some people than by others, and in the end, " nothing is lost."

The size of a group will vary, depending on the invitation given and the programme arranged by the host community. Small groups of between six and ten people are often best, because they are not so noticeable in the community they go to, and they may therefore learn more about the way of life than if changes were made to accommodate them. When a work-camp is planned a larger group of perhaps twenty or thirty people may be invited to join in. The Christians Aware Kenyan work-camps have often included large British groups working with equally large groups of Kenyan people.

Ideally a group should include people of different races, backgrounds and ages. It is sometimes possible to include people from two or three countries in a visit. When this can be arranged it is very interesting and valuable.

It is possible that people with medical problems or disabled people may apply to join a group visit. (Refer to the sections on disabled travellers and to the health section). It is wise to discuss the implications of their participation well in advance of the preparation of the group. The hosts should also be asked to share in the decision as to whether a disabled person should join a group visit. Sometimes hosts are pleased to welcome a disabled person, sometimes conditions are unsuitable.

The Group Leader

The group leader is first and foremost a member of the group who is also its enabler and the go-between for the visiting group and the hosts. The group leader has no special privileges, but is rather the last amongst equals, the person who makes sure his/her group members are fulfilled, comfortable and happy before seeking anything for him/herself.

It is vital that the group leader should know the group members well before the visit takes place. A good leader should know his or her group well enough to be able to delegate particular pieces of

Group Preparation

Photographs: Barbara Butler

work throughout the visit. One obvious role which may be delegated is that of treasurer for the group. It is very helpful if one person who is not the leader is responsible for the collection and payment of money. The person who will perform this role well is usually a fairly obvious choice.

Detailed knowledge of every group member may well be needed during a visit, so that any necessary communication with the hosts or local professionals may be swift and clear. The leader should always carry the names and addresses of contact people at home, details of passport numbers and dates and places of issue, insurance details, details of any illnesses or special needs, and, for most travel in the developing world, the blood groups for every member of a group. The section of this book on 'Health and Travel' will be especially useful for group leaders. If someone does become injured or fall ill during a visit it is important for the leader to make careful notes to pass on to a doctor or nurse. This is especially important if the group is in an isolated place, when it will take time to reach a medical centre. In the very unlikely event of a group member dying during a visit the leader must inform the high commission or embassy as well as contacting the insurance company. A decision must also be made about how and when to inform the family. It may also be necessary to safeguard the belongings of the person who has died, and to deal with the trauma of the other members of the group.

The leader should be aware of the group members' religious needs, interests, hopes and dreams. This may be achieved in many interesting ways in the preparation time, including role plays and discussions. The group leader must at all times protect the members of the group and individual members within it. Members will always benefit from reminders about the need to keep their money safe for instance. The leader may have to remind everyone of the value and equality of every person. This is sometimes hard to do when the group includes people of all ages. The leader will have to find time to listen to every person in a group and to have the patience to deal with any problems of antagonism between group members by struggling for understanding and reconciliation when necessary.

The group leader is the go-between and must therefore not only be sensitive to the needs, hopes and dreams of his/her group, but also to those of the hosts. It is sensible for the leader to be in contact with hosts well before a visit, through e-mails, letters and even telephone calls. Ideally the leader should have been to the host country to meet the hosts before becoming a leader, but this is not always possible. Regular communication is the next best, and essential, thing. Once the visit begins, hosts must naturally be kept informed on all issues which arise within a visiting group.

Awareness raising, especially about cultural differences, is essential as part of the preparation of any group. The leader must protect the hosts when necessary, and work hard to negotiate between the visitors and the hosts when expectations clash. Culture clashes must, if they arise, be faced and discussed openly by visitors and hosts. The visitors must be encouraged to adapt whenever possible, but common sense is necessary because sometimes people cannot fit completely into a new culture. This may sometimes be most obvious and painful where food and drink are concerned. Hosts may need help to understand this. Visiting groups sometimes have to be made aware by their leader of the enormous effort the hosts have put in to welcome them. This effort may be different from the effort the visitors would have made, but it is no less valuable. For example, in some cultures all the preparation for a visit is done at the last minute and also throughout the visit. Visitors may need help in understanding the timing of events. They may perhaps be encouraged to read, or to write diaries, or to hold a discussion whilst waiting for something to happen.

Being a group leader is a challenge, a struggle and a joy. A sense of humour can be a great help.

Spiritual reflection

A group leader's reflection on her preparation for a pilgrimage

This reflection is valuable as an insight into the pilgrimage to Mount Kailash, (Tibet), itself, but most importantly here it is an example of the detailed preparation this particular group leader made for her journey and her role.

'Whilst preparing myself to take a group of travellers to Mount Kailash, I have been musing on what it must be like to be a true pilgrim. In the dictionary a pilgrim is defined as 'one who travels to a distance to visit a sacred place,' whilst the word in Tibetan, '*gnas skor ba*' is translated as 'one who goes round a sacred place.' In these definitions I am a pilgrim, but have I prepared myself physically, mentally and spiritually for such an arduous journey? And do I have the right motivation?

Pilgrimage as a devotional exercise is one of the main characteristics of all the world's major religions. It is primarily a devotional and penitential act performed in order to accrue merit and overcome sin, with an underlying genuine desire to benefit all mankind. In Tibet pilgrimage is an essential practice of the lay people. Although banned by the Chinese authorities in the 60s and 70s, it has been re-instated and pilgrims are once again setting off on their spiritual journeys across the sacred landscape.

Tibet is a country imbued with great spiritual significance and therefore has an abundance of pilgrimage sites. These power places (*gnas chen*) are determined initially by their geomantic locations; that is a divined place of perfect harmony within the elements of the landscape. Thus the sanctity of a site is largely derived from its special physical characteristics, rather than from a shrine erected there.

According to this definition, there are numerous mountains, lakes, rivers and caves endowed with special properties. But there is also the indigenous Tibetan belief that these are the abodes of local deities and should be venerated as such. Mountains are particularly important, as in Tibetan mythology heavenly beings used them as vehicles to enter the world. And the first seven kings of Tibet are believed to have descended onto these mountains, by means of a sky rope. Mountain passes signify an altar below a mountain peak, so pilgrims make offerings of *mani* stones and *khatas* not only in gratitude for a safe crossing, but also because of the sanctity of the place.

Pilgrimage sites of deep significance are those associated with the lives of saints, ascetics and historical figures (ie. the meditation caves of Guru Rinpoche and Milarepa). When a site becomes a repository for a sacred object, it is then consecrated, thereby imbuing that place with greater spiritual power. The significance of a *chorten* is therefore not only as a representation of the Buddha-mind, but also a consecrated container of sacred relics – often of one specific holy person.

In order for the pilgrim to be inwardly in tune with his or her spiritual journey many devotional acts must be performed. Chief amongst these are circumnambulation, prostration, and the making of offerings. Circumnambulation is the clockwise walk of devotion around a sacred place, usually accompanied by the recitation of mantras. Prostration is the humble act of obeisance often performed in repetition around the *khora* circuit. And the making of offerings is an expression of gratitude and veneration to the deities within the sacred space. Offerings include *khatas* butter, *tsampa* and incense. Sources of worship are sacred objects and deities specific to a particular site. There are also those phenomena known as *ranjung* or that which has

There may be dangerous obstacles and hazardous situations along the way for any pilgrim

'spontaneously arisen.' This could be the rough image of a Buddha on a rock which has occurred without the aid of a human hand, or more frequently the hand and footprints of a guru. Finally, there is the sacred person, be it a monk, yogi, *tulka or ngakpa*. The blessings bestowed on a pilgrim by such a person are exceedingly powerful, as this transmission comes direct from the spiritual heart of the power place.

The pilgrims who make this arduous journey are of varying levels of spiritual attainment; for the *sanyasi* who has renounced everything, it is the ultimate journey to enlightenment, but to the more casual pilgrim it is a means of accruing merit in the hope of a better rebirth. For all of them, there are dangerous obstacles and hazardous situations along the way – for in a sense there is no gain without pain.

I consider myself to be a casual pilgrim who has prepared only partially, but I shall endeavour to be a mindful one. I must remember to pack blister plasters, but also an abundance of faith, perseverance and devotion.'

Going in a Group with Christians Aware

Christians Aware group visits and exchanges flow from a primary aim of the organisation, to develop multi-cultural understanding and friendship in a spirit of sharing so that a new focus and energy is generated for action towards human development and wholeness. Christians Aware works with members of other faiths, seeking to listen and learn.

The visits are distinctive in their emphasis upon the spiritual, upon encounter, using all our faculties. They offer a multi-faceted sharing amongst people in different cultures in places near and far. They help people to understand and respect each other and also to celebrate differences and see true unity in diversity. Not least, the visits help the hosts to be heard, and their views heeded, in a crowded, often very competitive, multi-racial and multi-cultural world.

Journeys taken 'with awareness' involve a deepening spiritual rapport between the travellers and the hosts. There are, both in sublime and very ordinary ways, truly inspirational, exhilarating delights and surprises to be had on a journey through God's creation in which both visitors and hosts joyfully share discoveries with each other. No wonder many people yearn to regain what is lasting, wholesome and true.

Regardless of distances covered or "sights' seen, quality time and relationships are of the essence: each Christians Aware visit usually lasts 2-3 weeks. Here inevitably there is some compromise between availability and budgets and the need for guests to spend enough time with hosts. The basis of the visit is mutual learning, in which the visitors are firstly, learners and respecters of the host culture rather than cultural imperialists. This applies especially to people from the so called "developed" or "rich" countries visiting communities in the "poor" or "two thirds world". But the principle of reciprocity and mutual regard applies world-wide.

Often the best ways of sharing and learning together are through shared activities of various kinds, for example conferences, work camps, exchanges between churches or dioceses and involvement in local community projects. The scope is very wide here, but the crucial starting point for a visit must always be an initiative, and invitation, from the hosts. Such proposals for a visit, and some outline ideas for its aims and content, may arise through contacts made at conferences, colleges or on earlier visits and exchanges between individuals in the host group and the leader of the proposed visiting group. Whenever possible, CA groups comprise people with a range of backgrounds and interests which is good for rapport between visitors and hosts.

However, while curiosity may prove a big part of the motive for tour members to join a visit to particular country/ place/ community, the "human zoo" syndrome must at all costs be avoided at all stages in the programme. This means that in every visit or exchange close attention must be given to preparation on the part of group members and hosts, and to opportunities during the visit for visitors and hosts (separately and together) to reflect on the appropriateness of the programme, and also to write a proper evaluation after the visit.

Wherever possible, visits and exchanges should not be "one off" events, but intended as part of a series of visits and exchanges, perhaps over several years. In this way, a deeper mutual understanding and respect, caring and co-operation can be developed. However, political events may work to compromise this ideal in certain instances. Moreover, under no circumstances should visits be suggested, or visit programmes arranged, or contacts made which will in any way place the hosts in a difficult, or even dangerous situation. Again, our "cue" in planning and managing the visits should primarily be taken from our hosts.

This is not to say that difficulties and tensions will not arise: they can, and they will, on every visit: yet by meeting such problems in discussion together – and this includes letters, e-mails, faxes and sometimes phone calls before the visit – many would be problems may be avoided, and such difficulties as do arise may be seen by both tour members and hosts on a creative "learning curve."

In any visit, group members and hosts will start out with their perceptions – even prejudices! about each other, and their own expectations of the visit. Close heed to the information and education of these perceptions and expectations before, during and after the visit for all involved is crucial to the removal of as much prejudice and misunderstanding as possible and for the inculcation of creative and responsive attitudes to each other. This is never easy, and there is bound to be misinformation, misunderstanding and mistakes. If, however, these can be resolved in the preparation stage, or as soon as possible at the start of the visit, much greater mutual benefit will ensue.

The difference between Christians Aware visits and many conventional types of holiday is that between pilgrimage and tourism. Rather than trying to see, do, "consume" and "commoditise" as many people, places and cultures in the shortest time possible (this is a process in which natural curiosity becomes more like voyeurism which de-humanises) we should seek to be open to cultural adventure, embracing some " reasonable" measure of risk with a willingness to be more "vulnerable" and less cocooned by the cult of celebrating modern, Western conveniences!

In all this, patience and a healthy sense of humour are vital. Humour is God's joyous, gracious deflater of hubris and release from tension and embarrassment! The true traveller, if only inwardly, soon learns when to laugh at him/ herself and with others (but never at others, notably when local culture shuns "loss of face"). Humour is the best medicine in many, though perhaps not all, difficult situations! For travel is always far more than an activity: it is an attitude of the spirit and of prayer, a journey of the heart, mind and will. The challenge is to be "open".

Paradoxically, it is through being in this position of "hazard", even knowing weakness, hassle and uncertainty, and through delightful surprises, spontaneity and sharing of both special and ordinary things that the real joys of encounter and mutual enrichment are often found. For our God is God of the unexpected, and true travel, as indeed life as a whole, is ultimately all about discovering, building and /or restoring relationships in all sorts of ways. In other words, we need to shun travel that is in the spirit of the archetypal wanderer and fugitive Cain, and embrace that of the true traveller and spiritual pilgrim seen in Abraham. G.K Chesterton, the 20th century writer, once summed up the contrast very succinctly if perhaps a little over-simply:

"The tourist comes to see what (s)he wants to see: the visitor comes to see what is there."

Clearly, for a variety of reasons, not everyone among the hosts or the visitors will be able or willing to enter into this spirit of pilgrimage all at once. Personalities, experiences and responses differ, and it is often for most of us many years before (as eloquently described by Laurens Van de Post, in one of his books):

> "We truly become pilgrims, travelling with the mind-set that Jesus or Paul and their companions must have had on their journeys two millennia ago".

And, come to think of it, Abraham, over 2000 years before then had quite a few testing experiences on his way, through which he came to receive more of God's promises and blessings.

Travel in a spirit of pilgrimage, whether in a "religious" or "secular" context, flows from a prayerful wonder at God's glory, creativity and amazing gifts of grace, and a responsive attitude of gratitude. Real travel, as part of life's journey which itself is a form of pilgrimage, has much in common with true wor(th)ship. Both are challenging and transforming of ourselves and of others in as far as we are really open to new experiences.

Despite our pride and waywardness, God still lovingly invites us to be what He made us to be – His partners in creating and renewing all things. In accepting, we become travellers in faith and in love. We discover the wonderful, the mysterious and miraculous, and gain a profound sense of the numinous, often in the most prosaic of moments. As we do this, we can know the beauty and delights of being ourselves wondrously changed and seek to encourage others to be likewise.

If you decide to contact Christians Aware please refer to the reference section at the end of the book.

Visiting Areas of Special Interest

'A few hours of mountain climbing turn a villain and a saint into two rather
equal creatures.'
Nietzsche

It is possible that our travels will take some people into countries offering special interests such as wildlife, art, history, sports and so on. Maybe we are already an expert in one or more area of special interest and will be well aware of where to go and how to create a good experience. We do not aim in this book to provide detailed information on specialist visits, though we do include suggestions for visiting places of historical interest, wildlife areas and for those who enjoy railway journeys. Our reference section may help those of us who are not experts and who wish to try something new or to develop a special skill or insight.

Every country offers historical interest, nature, music, architecture and dance. Those with a special interest in people and their faith and culture may ask Christians Aware for help with ideas and perhaps with the visit itself. Christians Aware visits often include meetings and work with people of other faiths, in the Middle East, in Japan, Mauritius, India and Sri Lanka. In India and Sri Lanka the visitors are guests of multi-faith communities and are invited to centres of dialogue and of practical development work. A section on visits to people of faith follows.

If adventure as well as spiritual experience is sought, or even adventure for its own sake, then the main qualification must be flexibility and a sense of humour, for after all the preparations have been made things will rarely go strictly according to plan. One person wrote about an exciting expedition to the Mount Elgon National Park on the border between Kenya and Uganda, when much of the time was taken up in

'...pushing the bus through the rain forest. We are off, sliding round the creepers. Splat! Champion fall in elephant dung...back to the bus. It's stuck in thick, red mud...The bus slides into the ditch and out of the ditch...Down the mountain, through the forest, passing villages, laughing children...'

Mountain climbing is a wonderful activity for the fit and adventurous. It is also perhaps the most unpredictable sport. Another Christians Aware group member wrote that:

"Climbing Mount Kenya was a very exciting and enjoyable experience for us Kenyans and for our visitors from Britain. At Met Station we lodged and that evening we had a chance to see some buffaloes, very dangerous animals...we were awake at 5.00.am and we walked through the bamboo forest, the mountain pasture and then the moorland...we had difficulty in breathing, the higher we climbed the steeper and tougher it was becoming. We slept at Makinder Camp, at 14,200 feet above sea level...breakfast was at 2.45 am and we walked with torches. It was very quiet with only the throbbing of the icy water and it was steep and slippery because of the snow. After a two hour climb there was silence and the thumping of boots. Cold, dry and chilly winds at the top of the mountain made many of us start and wish we had been left behind. Our faces, fingers and toes froze, making it hard to walk. We were in fear of sliding and we tried to make it with both legs and hands until at last we stepped onto Point Lenana, 16,335 feet above sea level."

We include an extract from "Touch the Earth" a self portrait of a true naturist, a lover of nature. It is a reminder of how vital it is to respect and come to love the special places we visit.

> 'He loved the earth and all things of the earth, the attachment growing with age. The
> old people came literally to love the soil and they sat or reclined on the ground with
> a feeling of being close to a mothering power. It was good for the skin to touch the

earth and the old people liked to remove their moccasins and walk with bare feet on the sacred earth. The birds that flew in the air came to rest upon the earth and it was the final abiding place of all things that lived and grew. The soil was soothing, strengthening, cleansing and healing.

That is why the old Indian still sits upon the earth instead of propping himself up and away from its life-giving forces. For him, to sit or lie upon the ground is to be able to think more deeply and to feel more keenly; he can see more clearly into the mysteries of life and come closer in kinship to other lives about him.

Kinship with all creatures of the earth, the sky, and water was a real and active principle. For the animal and bird world there existed a brotherly feeling that kept Lakota safe among them and so close did some of the Lakota people come to their feathered and furred friends that in true brotherhood they spoke a common tongue.

The old Lakota was wise. He knew that man's heart away from nature becomes hard; he knew that lack of respect for growing, living things soon led to lack of respect for humans too. So he kept his youth close to its softening influence.'

When popular destinations are chosen, such as Canada, Brasil, Australia, India, Thailand, and Kenya it is vitally important for the traveller to look behind the scenes and to be aware of the issues the people face and the conditions some of them are living in. Travellers may so easily be shielded from the reality of life. One way of avoiding this is to meet local people and to learn about their country from them. If you would find this hard to do on your own you could ask Christians Aware or one of the other organizations in the General Reference Section to point you in the right direction. It is vital to be aware of the indigenous people, for example the Inuit of Canada, the Yanomami of Brasil, the Aborigines of Australia. It is easy to find out about indigenous people by asking 'Survival International' for help. We include their address in the reference section at the end of the book.

A visit will be so much more worthwhile if there is both careful planning and preparation, including relevant reading and perhaps a focus on a special interest or concern, for example; meeting aborigines, talking with people of other faiths or enjoying time with a local family. The journey experience may then lead to greater awareness.

What you may want to Experience

If you are a traveller looking for interesting, satisfying, exciting new experiences you may find this section useful. The suggestions given here are merely a selection. The information is set out under simple headings, you may not find everything you need to know but we hope this will give you enough to make a start. For more details go to good guidebooks and travel web sites.

Historic Sites

Old civilisations provide endless interest to the traveller: if you feel you would enjoy this particular experience, these areas may be the ones to investigate

Mexico

San Miguel de Allende is a colonial town with many attractive houses and churches. It is full of artistic interest with painting, pottery, drama, music and literature.

Palenque is a Mayan site in a jungle clearing. There are some beautiful buildings including the Temple of Inscriptions, a stepped pyramid with an 25 metre tunnel leading to a crypt containing the sarcophagus of a 7th Century Mayan king.

Chichen-Itza is a very impressive Mayan site. You can find the reclining sculpture of the Toltec rain god. Remains of the Mayan civilisation are to be found throughout the Southern part of Mexico. Other sites in Mexico are to be found in: Tikal, Tulum, Uxmal and also in Guatemala, Belize and Honduras.

North America

In Quebec, Canada you will find the only walled city north of Mexico.

In Massachusetts, USA those who enjoy drama can see actors recreating the life and times of the first permanent colony and native American encampment in New England. There is an historical theme park and visitors can go aboard the Mayflower II, a reconstruction of the ship that brought the original settlers from England in 1620.

South America

Cuzco and the Urumbumba Valley, Peru. For people interested in the Inca civilisation, Cuzco offers plenty of sites, from there it is possible to travel to Machu Picchu.

Ouro Preto, in Brasil is a beautiful town founded in 1711, there is much to see here and it is a good base for further travel. Also, Salvador in the Norde Este has fine colonial buildings.

Africa

Egypt, Mali, Tanzania and Zimbabwe are countries well worth looking into for historical visits. Though Egypt is well known for its vast temples and inspiring history, it often forgotten that a number of other countries in Africa offer fascinating old towns, mosques, palaces and bazaars. There are many reminders of colonial days, especially in or near coastal towns or ports.

In Ethiopia Lalibela has 11 extraordinary medieval churches carved out of red volcanic rock. In these churches are beautiful frescoes and elaborate carvings. The churches are connected by a system of tunnels and passageways. Good times for a visit are in January and at Easter.

Asia

Mohenjodaro, Pakistan. Is a wonderful, impressive site of a civilisation dating from 2600-1800 BC.

Khajuraho, India.has 10th and 11th Century temple complexes which offer many sculptures and divine mythological subjects from the Hindu Chandela dynasty.

Hue is Vietnam's most beautiful city. There is the chance to sail up the Perfume river and see the moated citadel and join in the vibrant life of the population.

The Great Wall of China, Simatai, China is 1,400 miles long, and 13 ft wide, most of the wall is from the 14th-16th centuries. Simatai is probably the best place to visit and there are very impressive views of the mountains.

Xi'an, China has the Army of terracotta warriors. There is the large underground mausoleum of China's first emperor who died in 210BC. So far about 7,500 life-size soldiers have been unearthed, an amazing sight.

Nara in Japan is an ancient city offering many shrines, pagodas gardens and temples. The Buddha Hall contains the world's largest Buddha statue.

Europe

Pompeii, Italy is a site not to be missed. This remarkable historic site shows lifestyles up to AD49 frozen in time. It gives the visitor a chance to re-assess the modern world and know more about the people who lived and worked in the town of Pompeii.

Delphi, Greece. This is a wonderful place at the foot of Mount Parnassos where you will see a 4th Century BC temple to Apollo. There is a theatre and a stadium where the Pythian games were played.

Knossos in Crete has the remains of the Minoan civilisation of 3000-1100 BC.

Segovia in Spain is set on a rock, there is a beautiful castle, palace and a Gothic cathedral.

Mont St. Michel in France. The bay of St. Michel has a rocky island with a medieval abbey on the summit. Since the eleventh century some modifications have been put in giving an interesting mixture of styles including the nineteenth century church spire.

Petrodvorets, Russia has a beautiful parkland with an imperial palace built in Baroque style. Petrodvorets was built by Peter the Great and there is a system of beautiful fountains, cascades and waterways leading to the sea.

Rock of Cashel, Ireland. The town of Cashel in county Tipparary has a dramatic limestone outcrop some 109 m. high. On the top is a group of medieval ecclesiastical ruins including a bishop's palace, St Patrick's cathedral and a 12th century chapel.

Visiting historic sites is rather like opening a window to glimpse past civilisations. The traveller experiences a feeling of wonder and awe at the achievements of humankind: it enables one to assess modern life-styles and, in particular, modern architecture. Standing at the foot of a pyramid in Egypt, walking down a street in Pompeii, staring at the terracotta warriors puts the passage of time into perspective and perhaps brings new respect for the wonders of the world and the need for their preservation.

Photographs: Ailsa Moore, Alison Lyons, Barbara Butler

Wildlife Adventures for the Traveller

There are some excellent places to visit to see wildlife and appreciate the beauty of other inhabitants of our planet. It is important that all travellers take the utmost care when venturing into the territories of wild animals. Respect for conservation and the privacy of other species will result in enormous pleasure and the thrill of seeing nature at its best.

If you are thinking of travelling to wildlife parks, do become aware of all the factors that have gone into the setting up and running of these areas. As Survival International tells us, some of these parks have been set up at the expense of tribal people; the tourist wins and the tribal people lose. It is so difficult to balance the needs of wildlife, local people and tourists, it is the tourist who brings in the money, the responsible traveller can do things to re-set the balance of benefits between visitors and local people. Find out all you can about the areas you wish to visit before you go and when you are there, offer support by using advice from the organisation that knows the local situation. Pass on your knowledge to others and help to form or support a pressure group that will ensure a sustainable future for the local people and the wildlife of this planet.

People understandably believe that nature reserves protect endangered species, but the fact remains that putting a fence around an area containing wildlife does not always protect in the way hoped for. It is becoming increasingly obvious that the social conditions for the people living outside the reserves is of greater importance to the survival of the animals than the building of perimeter fences. The people living outside reserves need to have an economic interest in the survival of the animals, the way this is achieved is open to question and in many areas not resolved, a clash of interests can produce complex ethical problems. All travellers to wildlife reserves should be aware of these issues.

Here are just a few suggestions of places to visit.

North America	Wood Buffalo National Park in Canada offers a large number of species including lynx, buffalo, bears and a number of birds. This lovely wilderness can best be seen by canoe.
	Yellowstone National Park, Wyoming,USA- and Everglades National Park in FloridaUSA offer an abundance of wildlife.
South America	Podocarpus National Park in Equador is a place needing more protection from poachers and loggers, there is plenty to see under rather rough conditions. Visitors might look carefully to see what environmental help is needed.
	Manu Biosphere Reserve in Peru is excellent for bird species, has high altitudes and offers plenty of mammals including the jaguar and otters. Ecotourism is encouraged
	Pantanal, Brasil is a large area where the visitor has the chance of seeing animals wandering freely, it is possible to travel by boat or on horseback.
Europe	Lemmenjoki National Park, Lapland is a vast area, forested with rivers and hills. There are brown bears, lynx, moose and, of course, reindeer. In the Netherlands, the Waddenzee has a huge population of birds, waders, wildfowl, swans: excellent for keen bird watchers. Kisbalaton Reserve, together with Lake Balaton in Hungary is another excellent place for the birdwatcher. There is also Danube Delta in Romania, facilities here are not very good, but it is an unspoilt part of Europe.

Africa and Asia	offer plenty of opportunities to see wildlife. These continents are home to some of the world's most endangered species and some areas may also hold certain risks for the traveller. It is essential to check with embassies before travelling to countries such as Rwanda.

The following areas are of special interest and importance: Abuko Nature Reserve, Gambia. Tsavo, Kenya. Ngorongoro Crater, Tanzania. Bwindi National Park, Uganda. Kruger National Park, South Africa. Bird Island, Seychelles. Kaziranga National Park, Assam, India, Sundarbans, Wildlife Sactuary, India. These areas have tigers, bears, elephants, crocodiles etc. Tigers are threatened and increasingly rare. Khao Yai National Park in Thailand is a very interesting place to visit with a large variety of wildlife to see, though it is better to go with a guide. |
| **Australia** | Eungella National Park offers many beautiful and very spectacular areas, the wildlife is varied and includes kangaroos, possums, pythons and the ever interesting duck-billed platypus. |
| **New Zealand** | Otago Peninsular and Catlins Forest Park offer sights of penguins, seals, sea lions and a variety of birds and plants.

Always in the minds of conservationists and biologists are the Galapagos Islands off the coast of Equador. This area is very special and protected. Ecotourism here is strictly controlled, the environment is unique and fragile. There are the giant tortoises to be seen, and also iguanas, sperm whales and tropical fish. This is a place for the real enthusiast, but tread gently. |

Railway Journeys

If you are interested in experiencing the thrill of seeing breathtaking scenery, colourful landscapes, coast lines, shear drops and more in the comfort of a railway carriage then consider the following selection:

South America. Guayaquil to Quito, Ecuador. reaching an altitude of over 11,000 feet. Central Railway, Peru. The highest railway in the world, an exciting experience but often closed.

North America. Coast Starlight, USA, very much a coastal journey of some 1,300 miles.

Europe. Flam Railway, Norway, spectacular views and very steep.

Spain. Andalusian Express, a sightseeing journey, beautiful countryside views of villages and olive groves.

Switzerland. Glacier Express, a journey through the Swiss Alps, many tunnels and bridges and hairpin bends.

Africa. Marrakech Express, Morocco, a trip through the desert to Casablanca and along the coast The Blue Train, South Africa, visions of wildlife, desert and the Victoria Falls. Kenya Railways includes the beautiful journey, a section through a game park, to Mombassa on the coast.

Asia. Madras to Udagamandalam, India – an attractive journey, rural and dramatic. Darjeeling Himalayan Railway, India, a UNESCO heritage site, high climbs and dramatic views. Eastern and Oriental Express – Thailand and Malaysia, a long journey of over 1,000 miles, comfortable travel through jungles, plantations and farmlands.

Australia. Indian-Pacific, three days of travel from Perth to Sydney, a superb journey of space and mountains.

New Zealand. Trans-Alpine Express. a short journey of contrasts from east to west on South Island.

It is always wise to check whether the railways are open before you set out.

We believe the focus of travel should be on the people rather than the place

Visiting Specially Sensitive Parts of the World

'The greatest pleasure I know is to do good by stealth and to be found out by accident'.
Charles Lamb.

We have called this book "Go to the People" because we believe the focus of travel should be on the people rather than the place. It is through communicating, sharing, understanding and working together that people can bring about a happier, healthier, more friendly world. As a traveller you can contribute towards this goal. So let us go to the people with our eyes, ears, minds and hearts open; so that we become able to share an infectious enthusiasm for life wherever we go. If you choose to visit a part of the world where people have suffered conflict, famine, natural disaster or some other destructive event, you will have an opportunity to hear the stories of the local people and gain from them some of the spiritual strength that enabled them to survive. This meeting with those who live simple yet rich lives can be a wonderfully rewarding experience for both visitor and host. It can be a way of breaking through the boundaries of traditional tourism and coming into contact with feelings not experienced before. This leaves you with a new understanding of the power of human endeavour. If you would like to travel into this special world, then read on.

Once you have chosen to undertake one of these special journeys, it is important to plan and prepare carefully. You should be very aware of your motives, bearing in mind that travellers visiting merely as sightseers can be unwelcome in places where people have suffered a great deal. It is best to keep a low profile going gently, quietly and kindly, allowing people to talk if they wish to. It is best not to probe into sensitive subjects or seem to be critical. Travelling with awareness means knowing and appreciating the history and culture of the people and the places you visit. Our book aims to give plenty of references and information about different parts of the world. Please use this information, write away for leaflets and read some of the wonderful books that give inspiration and insight into the travel experience.

You are now ready to undertake your journey so here are some thoughts and ideas that may help you on your way. You may often have heard tourists complain about being besieged by beggars, but remember that as a traveller, you are not just a tourist and you will know that often visitors are the only source of income to many of the local people. Those who have been displaced from their homes because of war, natural disaster, and political or religious instability may have lost everything including members of their family. People in this situation often don't ask for money though they desperately need it, so how do you deal with this? It is helpful to be prepared beforehand. Avoid showing any unnecessary form of wealth. Expensive watches large overfull handbags and expensive clothes tend to show superiority and this is unkind and likely to cause problems.

In making your decision about whether to give to beggars or not it is wise to consult your host, if you have one. Alternatively a local church or development group may be able to advise you. It is often wiser to give to a group working with beggars, street children and other very poor people, so that many people are helped rather than just the few you might have given your money to.

If a local person does a small favour for you then you may wish to offer reward, but this can sometimes be seen as an insult so go with awareness. Often just acknowledging and talking with people, even without knowing their language, works wonders and they feel cared about.

If you find yourself staying with local hosts you may find your host too proud to accept payment. If this is the case try to carry small gifts from your own country that you can give in return for hospitality. It is often a good idea before accepting hospitality, to ask if you may share some of the cost, this can ease things when you leave. It may often be good idea, instead of offering payment, to buy some

A refugee family from Bosnia setting up home under a tree

Photographs: Ailsa Moore

Refugees in a temporary camp show courage

really needed item for a child or older person in the family, it may be possible to treat the family to a meal out. Some people, children in particular, like having their photographs taken but be sure to ask first and be sensitive to any lack of enthusiasm. Some cameras can produce instant prints; these can be a source of great fun and joy. One of the best icebreakers is to share family photographs, take with you photographs of your children, parents, pets, they have universal appeal. If your host offers you some treasured item as a gift, always accept it with dignity and pleasure. It is always a wonder to those of us who have so much that people with so little are so generous. The more we have the harder it seems to be able to give it away. Being a good guest takes a great deal of awareness and sensitivity and sharing someone's home can be a thrilling and warming experience.

It is always wise to collect all the information you can about a place before deciding to go there, especially if the place has had problems. Seek advice from people and organisations with experience of the country and ensure it is safe to go there and travel around. If you do travel to a country that has suffered problems of any kind please be guarded in your conversation and avoid confrontation. It is often easier to travel in small groups or even singly. Sometimes large groups of people may seem threatening and less friendly. Read Dervla Murphy's "One Foot in Laos," which is included in the book list. Think carefully about why you want to visit the chosen country and what you may be able to do to assist the people there. These exercises are rewarding in themselves, and on arrival in the country they can make all the difference to the enjoyment and the productivity of the visit. If you can learn some of the local language please do, this will endear you to your hosts and bring relaxing amusement to all.

When you return home, spend some time assessing your experiences and reflecting on impressions you have of the people and the place. This can make the whole venture so much more worthwhile. It is so useful to keep a simple diary and a note of the names of people and of their addresses, you will probably want to make contact again. We include a section on keeping a diary in Chapter Two. A thank-you card from home can be so welcome to people who may have little contact with the outside world. They may also like to receive a copy of your diary and some photographs.

You may have witnessed poverty, illness, tears and destruction, but be sure, you will have brought great pleasure and hope to the people you met, and you yourself will feel challenged and uplifted by the experience.

Some parts of the world are so politically sensitive or dangerous of course that it would be unwise to visit them. If you are in any doubt it is always essential to carry out checks with the appropriate organisations and/or embassies. In the case of certain countries, for example Burma and Tibet, it is helpful to contact one or two of the organisations listed in the reference section at the end of the book. Embassies are the best contacts to make if you are in any doubt about safety. Travel to a country with conflict going on can prove to be very dangerous and you don't want to cause problems to anyone by travelling there.

Also carefully heed the latest advice posted on the UK Foreign Office web site. The details are given in the general reference section.

Preparing

Chapter Two

Preparing

'So it is in travelling: a man must carry knowledge with him, if he would bring home knowledge.'
Samuel Johnson

In this chapter we offer useful practical hints on how to prepare for a trip abroad and what essentials should be covered before leaving home.

Getting the best out of travel

The time spent in preparing for travelling is vitally important. The nature of your preparation will depend upon whether you are going alone, or in a family or in a group. Preparation should be arranged well ahead of the visit, and should include enough time for necessary vaccinations and other protective care to be given. If practicable, and especially when more than two or three people are travelling together, a residential weekend could be arranged. This need not be expensive if it is self-catering, and may sometimes, if the group is small, be organized in a member's home. The self-catering aspect of a residential weekend is an opportunity for a variety of people to become a group and to begin to learn how to work together. If a weekend of preparation is not possible, then a long day may be arranged, or two separate days. If you are travelling as a family or on your own you won't require the experience of a residential weekend.

Preparing for travel as a group

It will be beneficial if the preparation time before travel includes time for people to articulate their hopes and fears of the visit, and for these to be discussed and where possible dealt with. This may be tackled by people talking in twos and threes about themselves, their work and way of life, their families and anything else they see as part of their contribution to the visit. Language skills for example might be of use. It is useful after this session for the group leader to make a list of the particular skills and interests of the members of the group. It is important to identify musicians, artists and photographers. Someone may also like to take a tape-recorder on the visit. Time is also needed for people to listen to someone from the country they will visit, who may talk about the history, geography, culture, and current issues facing the country. This session may include a slide-show and use of maps. It is also helpful to include the experiences of members of any previous visits to the same place. Time must be given for the group leader to talk about the host community, and the detailed programme whilst also drawing out the expectations of the group. The host community may not be able to provide a programme before a visit takes place. In this case there should be discussion of why this may be so, including the fact that many communities live from day to day, having sufficient challenge in feeding themselves and their children. There may be the need for the travellers to be open and flexible, ready to face whatever is offered to them, realising that there will be so much more to learn in a community which is very different from their own. A practical session is essential when kit lists are made up, including lists of suitable clothes, and first aid. We include a kit list for visits to the tropics at the end of the book. The particular needs of individuals should be discussed. Some items may be shared by a group, including clothes pegs, washing lines and sewing kits. It is not wise for first aid items to be shared, except perhaps the sterile travelling pack recommended for tropical areas and especially in Africa because of the AIDS pandemic.

Photographs: Ailsa Moore & Barbara Butler

Be
Prepared

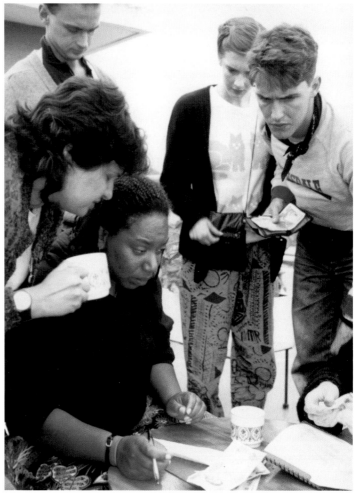

Preparation time may include walks, as an aid to the development of friendship and understanding, and role play on some of the situations which may arise during the visit.

The experiences of one group, when camping in the Kenyan Rift Valley, would be a good focus for a role play. The group set up the camp and then went for a walk only to return to the camp to find that baboons had been into the tents, and had eaten the toothpaste, pills, (those for constipation and those for diahorrea), and anything else they could find. They had also torn the tents. A more difficult and more usual situation might be one of culture clash between the visiting group and the hosts, and of how this might be tackled. One issue of culture which often arises when groups from the Western World visit communities in the Developing World is the issue of time. Western visitors do sometimes expect things to happen on time, whilst their hosts are much more relaxed. (See page 100 - "Time").

General preparation for every traveller.

It is vital that the preparation time for a visit should include discussion on the various hurdles travellers may face. One of these is the issue of changing money, which can be very difficult and time consuming. Following on from that is the issue of safety. It is wise to change money at the airport immediately after arrival in a country. Airport banks are normally quick and efficient. It is hard to decide whether to change a lot of money, and then have the problem of security, or to change a little, and then have to go to a bank later. The issue of how to carry money must be faced in advance of any visit and should be discussed carefully by group travellers. It is wise never to carry any valuables that are not essential to the journey. The essentials are cash, travellers' cheques, passport and perhaps a credit card. If travellers do not have a credit card they would be wise to take extra travellers' cheques for emergency use. The essentials should be hidden under a shirt, perhaps in a money belt and never left behind in a room or on the seat in a plane. Some people make a special small bag, which is supported by a shoulder strap and fits under the shirt, or under the pillow in a guest-house or train. Visible bags and purses are very vulnerable. The money needed for the day can be carried in a separate small purse.

It is important that travellers are always wary but not nervous when moving around in public places. This rule may also apply in public places in one's own country of course. In some countries of the Developing World however it is important to remember that money from the Western World will go a very long way and the temptation to pick pockets is therefore that much greater. It is possible that a child may be clothed and sent to school for what it costs for a person from the UK to make one journey. (This is worth thinking about when deciding how to thank host communities on returning home). It is wise to be especially alert if there is a disturbance of any kind, if someone bumps up against someone else or if there is an 'event' which could of course be staged. It is wise to be particularly careful when arriving in a new country for the first time, and especially when leaving the airport probably surrounded by new faces, including those who want to carry the luggage.

Preparation time should include discussion on keeping safe when moving around, especially when walking, in new environments. The discussion will obviously have different outcomes depending upon the country to be visited. However, whenever possible it is sensible to walk, because that is the only way to learn in depth and to be part of the community. If walking is considered dangerous alone or with a group of visitors, one way to walk may be to do so with local hosts who know their way around, and who will introduce visitors to the most interesting people and places. People should be alerted to the dangers of going alone into lonely places, including dark alleys and buildings. The dangers may be even greater if someone invites the traveller to go into a lonely or dark place.

Travellers should consider the many ways the precautions to take in order not to get lost during their travels; including taking a good map or maps with them, always knowing the address they are staying

Keeping safe when moving around does not always depend on the quality of the transport

at, and having it clearly written down. These seem to be very obvious precautions to take, but it is amazing how many people fail to do so, and sometimes they can't even tell a taxi driver where they are staying! Group members should make clear arrangements about where to meet if they split up for any reason. It is also a good idea for visitors to ask their hosts to draw them a sketch map of where they are staying, marking out streets, street corners and special land marks if they are staying in a town or city, and fields, trees, mountains etc. if they are staying in the countryside. Sometimes members of a group may be split up to stay in different homes, perhaps even in different villages. It is important then for everyone to have a list of names and addresses and simple directions and maps so that they can reach each other if necessary.

Resources for preparation should be considered, including book-lists, people to meet, and perhaps visits to relevant libraries and museums. It is helpful to write to the hosts, giving news of the visitors and of the preparation time. It is important to encourage travellers to share news of their proposed visit with their local church or community. This will give the local community an interest in the visit, and will also give the traveller(s) the opportunity to share experiences and new insights after the visit. It is possible that local communities may wish to sponsor a visit in some way.

A useful list of practical things to cover before leaving home

1   Is your passport up to date?

2   Do you require visas?

3   Do you need to take steps to cover any health needs? (Pick up the travel health guide from your post office).

4   Have you full insurance cover?

5   Check all flight times and know the time differences. Check air tickets in the countries you will visit.

6   Be sure to carry with you the names and addresses of the hotels etc. where you will be staying, including your own home address.

7   Be sure to leave all information with a friend or family at home. (Include insurance details, your will details, hotel contacts and any requests).

8   Make a will if you need to, it can be a great comfort just to know you have done it.

9   Check your cash arrangements.

10   Arrange homes for any pets you may have.

11   Check on your home and car security.

12   Buy maps and phrase books.

13   It can be a good idea to inform the police where to obtain a key.

14   Cancel the milk and papers.

15   Make a decision about your central heating.

16   Check the weight of your luggage before travelling.

17   Remove all sharp objects from your hand luggage.

18   Remember to lock the front door behind you!

See our kit list in Chapter Six.

Health and Travel

Travellers will rarely encounter serious health problems if they take simple precautions. Minor ailments such as stomach upsets or diarrhoea are more common when visiting countries that are unable to afford the same standards of public health as we have in Britain. But by paying more attention to staying healthy than you would at home, even these risks can be reduced to a minimum.

In preparation for your journey you should obtain a copy of the Department of Health booklet *Health Advice for Travellers* free from your post office or from the Health Literature Line on 0800 555 777. For 10 copies or more, apply to PO Box 77, London SE1 6XH, fax 01623 724 524 or e-mail doh@prolog.uk.com . For more detailed information, it is well worth purchasing *The Travellers' Good Health Guide* by Ted Lankester published by Sheldon Press and excellent value at £6.99 from bookshops or from InterHealth, 157 Waterloo Road, London SE1 8US, tel. 020 7902 9000 e-mail supplies@interhealth.org.uk. Read it before you go and take it with you. InterHealth also produces health information packs, sells medical supplies for travellers and they run a travel clinic. British Airways also run travel clinics around the country; the telephone number for details is 01276 685040.

Before you go

Three months before you go, tell your doctor or your practice nurse about your travel plans. Many practices provide print-outs of up to date travel advice. Your discussion should include:

a)   Any immunisations that you will need. There may be a charge for some of these. Children and expectant mothers have special requirements. For all countries outside Western Europe, North America and Australasia adults will require:
- Tetanus and diphtheria.
- Polio
- Typhoid
- Hepatitis A

  For some countries you will also need
- Yellow fever (with a certificate to show that you have had this)
- Meningococcal menigitis A and C

  For some places and specific circumstances immunising is advised against:
- Hepatitis B. This is only routinely needed for doing medical work or activities involving contact with bodily fluids. It takes 6 months to gain full protection.

- Tuberculosis immunisation (BCG) does not provide complete protection but it is a wise precaution in some countries if you mix socially with less advantaged people. Your doctor may test you to see if you are already immune.
- Rabies might be wise if you are likely to be exposed to wild or stray animals.
- Tick-borne encephalitis
- Japanese encephalitis

Remember to check the cost before having vaccines, particularly rabies vaccine.

b)   Anti-malarial medication.
- These medicines are an essential precaution for visitors to many countries (see list in *Health advice for Travellers*).
- They have to be purchased and some have to be prescribed by your doctor.
- A medication that prevents you from becoming ill is called a *prophylactic* drug.

- Expectant and nursing mothers have special requirements and so do children and those who suffer from epilepsy, liver and kidney disorders.
- **It is very important to begin anti-malarials at least 2 weeks before you set off and not to finish them until you have been home for 4 weeks.**
- The most suitable kind of anti-malarial varies with the part of the world being visited. **If the recommended anti-malarial is one that you have not taken before, it is wise to check that it suits you by starting it at least three weeks before travelling.** If you do react to one medication there are alternatives.
- Taking antimalarial medication does not guarantee total protection from malaria so if you feel unwell while you are away, always seek medical advice.

c) Mosquito Nets.

If you need anti-malarial medication, then using an insecticide impregnated mosquito net will further reduce the risk of catching malaria. A net will also protect you from being bitten by unwelcome nocturnal visitors on the wing or of the crawling variety. Nets come in single and double bed sizes and can be bought from outdoor/camping shops. Take some means of fastening it to a ceiling such as cup hooks and a small tool to insert this.

d) Other Night-time Precautions against Mosquitoes.

The vapour from mosquito coils or electrically powered vaporising mats deters mosquitoes. They are available in many destinations as well as here in Britain.

e) On-going Medical Problems.

If you have on-going medical problems such as asthma, diabetes or heart disease, do take written details about your condition. Contact details of a doctor who might be approached for further information may also come in handy.

f) Regular Medication.

If you normally take medicines or need injections at home:

- You need to be sure that you will have sufficient while you are away. There is a limit to the amount that your doctor can supply under the NHS before you go. If this is insufficient then your doctor may be able to guide you about the best course and further advice about availability abroad can be obtained from the manufacturer. In some countries your medicines may be expensive or unobtainable, so buying additional supplies before you go may be the only option.
- Always carry a note of the doses and the proper name of the medication; overseas pharmacists or doctors are often unable to recognise the British trade names of medicines.
- All medicines should be in the correctly labelled container from the chemist.
- It is wise to check that there are no restrictions on the transport of your medication out of the home country or into other countries. You can find this out from your doctor or check with the Home Office Drugs Branch (tel. 020 7273 3806) and the relevant Embassies.
- If you will need to change your clock more than and hour or two during the journey, check with your doctor about the times at which you will need to take your treatment. Generally speaking, you need not change your watch on the plane until you reach your destination and during the flight you can continue to take medication more or less according to your watch. At the destination, when you change your watch, if the time to the next dose is much shorter or longer than the normal interval between doses, you might need to add a dose or miss one out.
- If you have diabetes, Diabetes UK (tel. 020 7323 1531; e-mail info@diabetes.org.uk) supplies *Travel and diabetes,* a booklet that gives advice about insulin injections during travel, what to take and many other hints.

g)   First Aid.
It is sensible either to buy a kit or make up your own with adhesive dressings, antiseptic cream, insect repellent as well as some water sterilisation tablets. You may also want travel sickness pills, some sachets of oral rehydration powder, something to calm diarrhoea and ciprofloxacin antibiotic, useful for more severe diarrhoea but this last has to be obtained from your doctor (see section on diarrhoea).

h)   Emergency Kit.
Travellers to countries where sterile medical equipment may not be available can buy a sterile pack from the larger chemists in case you need injections or fluid replacement into a vein. If you are in a party you can share one of these packs.

i)   Medicines for More Remote Areas.
If you are going to be away from reliable medical facilities and pharmacies then you may want to take some basic medicines. You will need to discuss this with your doctor. Children, expectant and breast feeding mothers need special consideration. Details are given in *The Travellers' Guide to Good Health (see above).*

j)   A Doctor's Note.
A note stating that medication and an emergency kit is for personal use will prevent problems at customs.

k)   Other Items that Might be Hard to Find
These include tampons, contraceptives and contact lenses.

l)   Health Insurance.
Only a minority of countries outside the EEA has a reciprocal health care agreement with the UK and even reciprocal arrangements in the EEA will not cover all eventualities. *Health advice for travellers* and consumers organisations have useful advice and you could also consult your travel agent and insurer.

m)   Dental Health.
A check-up early enough to give time for treatment is wise.

n)   Blood group.
Take a note of your group if you have been told this.

On the journey
Some simple precautions include:

a)   On long-haul flights there is a small risk of developing blood clots in your leg veins. For passengers over 12 years of age taking one aspirin tablet before you set off reduces the chance of this happening. Drinking plenty of liquid is recommended but go easy on the alcohol, which can make matters worse. Moving your legs and going for a walk also helps to prevent stiffness as well as reducing the chances of clotting.

b)   If you need regular medicines or give yourself injections, you will be taking them on the journey at the times that you have already planned (see above). Be aware of time differences.

c)   It is a wise precaution to split essential medication into more than one item of luggage in case you and your cases are separated.

d)   Ear discomfort that may develop during landing can be avoided by sucking a sweet, swallowing or blowing out with the nostrils pinched.

When you are away

a)   Road Accidents.

Being knocked down or injured in a crash is more likely than catching a serious illness in most countries. So:

- It is vital to take care as a pedestrian.
- Reckless minibus driving is fairly common in some countries, so consider the risks involved if you use this kind of transport.
- If safer travel is not available by train or full sized bus, hiring a vehicle with a driver may be an affordable alternative, particularly if you are one of a group. If you do have your own driver, don't be reticent about asking him to slow down if you feel that the road conditions warrant this.

b)   Water.

- The amount that you will drink will rise if you travel to a hotter climate.
- In most developing countries the water contains more germs than are allowed in developed countries, and it is unfit for drinking or brushing teeth. The same applies to ice.
- Boiling for 5 minutes and then keeping the water in a scalded container usually makes it safe.
- If you staying for some time, a filter jug with a porcelain *candle* may be convenient, only slightly less safe than boiling and may improve the taste of the water. Some candles are impregnated with silver that kills germs; those that are not should be boiled once a week.
- Always remember to scald containers and for this reason metal ones may be preferable to plastic for carrying drinking water.
- Where boiling is not possible, you can add a sterilising tablet to the water and then wait for at least 20 – 30 minutes (1 – 2 hours in very cold conditions). Always follow the maker's instructions.
- If you are staying in someone's home, our experience is that they will understand your need to have boiled water, so don't hesitate to mention this.
- In many places shops sell bottled water that is usually safe. Sodas made by well-known multinationals are also usually safe.

c)   Food.

Rather more care is needed in developing countries.

- Wash your hands before handling food or eating.
- If you eat out ask the advice of local ex-patriots about safe restaurants.
- Fruit and vegetables are important constituents of your diet. Indeed fresh fruit and a different range of vegetables are some of the delights of living in the tropics. They are safe if you have peeled them or washed them yourself with boiled water. But when you are eating out only eat these items if they have been cooked thoroughly as they are a common source of food poisoning.
- It is also best to avoid bought ice creams, yoghurts and cheeses unless from a safe source and preferably pasteurised.
- It is important that meat and fish are cooked thoroughly.
- Avoid food that has been kept warm, cooled or reheated.
- In some parts of the world raw fish or shellfish are on offer but they may carry parasites.
- Eggs should be cooked until the yolk is hard.
- UHT milk is often available but if you dislike it or it cannot buy it, fresh milk should

be boiled for 5 minutes, and either kept in a fridge or drunk the same day.
- When you are a guest and are offered food that is likely to be risky in someone's home, you can say that the doctor (me!) has told you to avoid the item for personal health reasons.

d) **Anti-malarials.**
Many people find it difficult to remember to take medicines but putting them with your tooth kit helps and weekly medication is less easily forgotten if taken at the end or beginning of a week.

e) **Mosquito Nets.**
If your hosts do not supply a net, they are likely to understand your need to erect one and will allow you to do so – particularly if you can leave it behind!

f) **Hygiene.**
Microbes, parasites and insects love to share your space! Take care with personal hygiene. Frequent washing of clothes, wiping surfaces and keeping floors clean all pay dividends.

g) **Sunburn and Heat.**
In hot countries keeping out of the sun and wearing clothes and hats that shield the skin is generally the best protection. Sun cream should be used for skin where exposure is unavoidable. It is also important to drink enough when you are hot. If you are passing small amounts of dark coloured urine, step up your fluid intake.

h) **HIV/AIDS, Sexually Transmitted Diseases and Hepatitis B and C.**
None of these conditions are passed on through everyday social contact, kissing, coughs or sneezes, nor by insect bites, dirty food or crockery.
But they are distressingly common in many parts of the world. Treatment exists for most sexually transmitted diseases but there is no vaccine or cure for infection with the HIV virus that causes AIDS. Travellers are at risk of infection with HIV and also hepatitis B and C if we are exposed to:
- Unprotected sex with an infected person. Casual sex is very risky.
- Infected medical and dental equipment and anything else that pierces the skin such as tattooing.
- Transfusion of HIV infected blood.

If you think that any of these have happened, the only safe course is to seek urgent attention at the nearest centre that is able to offer reliable investigation and advice.

i) **Swimming.**
If you swim other than in a pool, seek authoritative local advice first. There may be a risk from tides, currents or flash floods. The bilharzia parasite is another hazard in many rivers and lakes in tropical countries, as this can penetrate the skin leading to illness.

j) **Diarrhoea.**
So-called Travellers Diarrhoea is a common experience when visiting developing countries. The risk can be minimised by following the water and food precautions given above. Episodes are usually short-lived and not incapacitating. Drink plenty of fluid. Drinking an Oral Rehydration preparation will ensure that you make up what you are loosing. Antibiotics are not advised for mild diarrhoea but where it persists and interferes with your programme, you may want to reduce the number of toilet stops by taking a one of the versions of loperamide that can be bought across the counter such as Imodium, Diareze or Diocalm Ultra. If the problem continues you could take two ciprofloxacin 250mg antibiotic

tablets as a single dose. You should seek medical advice if the diarrhoea still persists and at any time if you are unable to hold liquids down, you are becoming dry, your diarrhoea is blood stained, you have cramping pains or if you pass very large amounts of watery motion.

On your return home.
    a)   Remember to take antimalarial medication for four weeks.
    b)   If you become ill after you return, tell your doctor where you have been.
    c)   If you developed diarrhoea while away or on your return, take care in handling food and, if you do so professionally, tell your doctor and employer.
    d)   Make any health insurance claims as soon as possible.

Prevention not panic
If you now feel that going abroad is too dangerous, stop thinking about your health for a few days. Then read this chapter again and the precautions that are suggested should appear less threatening. Although minor illness is fairly common when visiting less developed countries, it is very rare for illness to overshadow the joy of new friendships and the thrill of experiencing new places and cultures. Bon voyage!

Taking Photographs

Most travellers, though not all, wish to make a photographic record of their experiences, perhaps for publication, to share with friends or to use when they give talks. Buying and processing film is expensive and it is therefore sensible to preserve the films as well as possible whilst travelling. It is helpful to invest in a lead bag to keep films in throughout a journey, and not just when you are passing through airport security barriers. The airport X Ray equipment will not destroy film but it may diminish the quality of the photographs. The lead bag is also useful in protecting the films from extreme heat or cold. A cheap alternative to the bag is to wrap new and used films in tinfoil.

If it is worth paying for the films then it is also worth paying a little extra to make sure they are developed well.

Before taking photographs think carefully about what you may use them for. Distant views are rarely useful for publishing purposes whereas close up pictures, of things and of people, are normally far more effective. Your family may wish to see you standing in front of every place you visit, and with every group you meet, but few other people will appreciate this.

Remember that photographs of people which are taken quickly, so that the subjects do not become self-conscious and line up in a formal and very boring row, are the most interesting and useful. However, in some cultures it is important to ask before taking photographs of people. This is especially true in Muslim cultures and countries. It will be easy to work out when to ask and when to take quick and very natural photographs. The choice of camera for the journey will determine how successful you will be in taking good natural photographs of people. A built-in zoom or a zoom attachment will help enormously, not only in taking natural close –up pictures, but also in framing the pictures well.

If you take photographs at high altitude remember there is more ultraviolet radiation, this will register on colour film as blue. The most generally useful lighting for mountain photography is side lighting. This brings out the texture and contours, and combined with some atmospheric haze to give an impression of depth, will bring out the 'feel' of a mountain. Back lighting from a high sun can produce dramatic effects. It can be worth experimenting a little before going on your travels, especially if photography is to play an important part in the journey.

Always take at least twice as many photographs as you will wish to use. In this way you will have choice and you will not, hopefully, be disappointed by the results.

It is usually wise to buy enough spare films before travelling. It can be difficult buying films in remote places. You may wish to have films developed before returning home but remember the processing may not be as good as at home.

"En largo camino paja pesa." (**On a long journey even a straw seems heavy**). Spanish proverb.

"In no part of photography can we indulge our personal preferences more than in our modes of travel. Within limits we can choose any way to carry equipment which suits us best. Well known photographers have carried their cameras in brief cases, shopping bags, rucksacks, custom made cases, ex-army ammunition boxes, around their waists or just in their pockets. There are some excellent aluminium cases with foam inserts, but sooner or later, one comes to the conclusion that a camera is intended to be ready for use at all times, and elaborate cases slow down the process.

For travel to base, rigid cases are the best answer. If possible, clear colour films out of the camera before the journey, always load films out of direct light. The main consideration for carriage of films is to keep them as cool as possible and dry, - particularly colour films. Freezer bags or cool bags can be very useful for this purpose. When carrying spare films be sure to store them away from heat and

A cup of tea would be nice. Sugar is available, but a spot of milk is dear. A responsible community member has prepared a zero grazing unit. Your heifer is providing milk for more than one family. In time you will be glad that you are returning a heifer calf to be a life saver for another family.

Should we take food for the journey? It will take 10 hours. Jam is expensive, sliced bread will do. We need to make a bargain for bananas and bread. Coke is a fixed price you must return the bottles.

To finish the fishpond we must dig a channel from the stream. Will the water syphon up hill? Maybe another route through crops, compensating the farmer would be best. We need pipes to go under the road. On Monday someone will go to look for them. Has anyone in town got pipes? They have, the next stage of the project will be finished.

JW.

One way of keeping a diary   © Julia Woodger

light.

Used with permission, from the book, "The travelling photographer" by Derek Widdecombe.

Keeping a Diary

Every traveller should try to keep a diary of his/her experiences, though the way this is done will vary greatly from person to person because it is important for this activity to be creative and hopefully enjoyable.

The first thing to decide is how the diary will be used. If it is to be a simple record for personal perusal and pleasure then it may perhaps be written in note form and accompanied by pencil sketches in a light and easy to carry notebook. Some travellers will prefer to create a beautiful record as they go along, with poems, stories, detailed descriptions and full colour paintings. This choice will depend upon the ability to carry and preserve the paints, crayons, books etc.

For children, keeping a diary can be a useful experience and also of great benefit when returning to school. Teachers often ask their pupils for an account of their holidays and sometimes the colourful well presented records may appear on parents evenings.

If the diary is to be published then the writer will obviously need to decide the purpose and his/her priorities before setting out on the journey. Research may need to be done before the journey begins, and this may determine the form the diary takes. An important decision will be whether to focus on people, places or events, because it will be impossible, in one journey and visit, to do everything.

A day from Kitty Campbell's February 2002 Bangladesh diary.

Quite a day! Breakfast at Taize Brothers, then visited their Centre for the Handicapped. Fascinating – carpet weaving – lovely rugs, and also boys making lovely cards - bought some. Physiotherapy room, basic social skills for children with learning difficulties, school, and " women's club", for chat, recreation, self esteem etc.

Then off to Garo festival at Pannihatta. Drove in microbus to Haluaghat, St Andrew's Mission. Found Angela had left earlier. Toilet stop there. Then 90 minute (nearer 2 hours) ride on rickshaw!!. I couldn't balance. Got in and "driver" immediately set off pedalling. Kept slipping off seat – it was tilted forwards. If I'd known, I'd have worn trousers rather than a long floaty slippery skirt! Eventually stopped and we got two – one each for Elisabeth and I. Much better – could get a grip – though still not exactly comfortable!

Got to Pannihatta. Had rice with meat. Climbed steep but short hill and looked over river into India. Lunch time at the festival. Due to start again at 2.00pm – eventually did at 3.10pm. We introduced ourselves, brought greetings – and then had to leave! Big marquee, with PA system – and youngsters' band.

Discovered no rickshaws available in Pannihatta – but Angela had kept hers there. Someone went off on motorbike to find one in next village, but eventually Rita and Elizabeth went back on the pillion of motorbikes, and I shared Angela's rickshaw. Got another half way because really too much for her "rickshaw wallah". Quite enjoyed it coming back – but not sure if I'll be able to walk tomorrow!

Microbus back to Mymensing. Late for service. Lovely meal with Naomi again. Chat with boy from Tripuri tribe in Chittagong hill tracks – wanted my address and says he'll write.

A few days from Philip Collin's November 2001 Vellore Diary

I arrived in Katpadi, on the outskirts of Vellore on Monday 12th November, 2001, having shared a taxi for the 120 km journey with two fellow "Christians Aware" travellers, Rena and Alan Partridge. Alan and Rena knew Vellore well, having spent four years of their lives there at the Christian Medical College and Hospital. Lydia, The Revd Christopher (her father), Paul (brother) and Anita (his wife), and dear little Sheryl (now eight months old) extended a great welcome to me. It soon became evident that " the gang" were coming to see me too – Silas, Aaron and Mythili. I left the house with Paul at about 10pm, and was taken to the Karigiri Leprosy Hospital, which was to be my accommodation base for the week.

I must admit at first to a feeling of "where on earth am I?" as I arrived at the guest house amidst the noise of crickets, bullfrogs and a kamikazi attack from mosquitoes, some eight kilometres in the country away from Katpadi.

On waking with the dawn the next morning I couldn't believe my good fortune. It was absolute heaven - beautiful countryside, birdsong, fresh air, sunshine, woodlands, and safe footpaths galore, just beckoning exploration. Having said that, they were not such inviting paths after dark, and the nightly excursion to the telephone (STD/ISD) passing a lagoon, with all the night noises you expect to hear in a "Tarzan" film, caused me to run there and back, making almost as much noise myself as the night creatures.

I visited the Katpadi Industrial Institute the next morning with The Revd.Christopher. The institute is a vast complex where young men who would otherwise not have the resources could learn particular skills. The main areas of learning were in electronics, electrical engineering, carpentry and metal craft. What was so admirable (and so un-British!) was the up-front way in which the Christian Faith is proclaimed throughout the Institute. It is faith in Christ that motivates the project, guides the staff and surrounds the students. There is an open policy on admissions; admittance to the institute is not dependant upon the entrant having a Christian faith. Nevertheless it is obvious that the faith of those who guide the project is infectious.

The major problem facing the Institute seemed to be one of finance. Some of the work, particularly the cane work, was exquisite, and would have done justice to Harrods, (which I suggested). Work, for which they were prepared to sell for £300 could fetch at least double that amount in the States or Western Europe, thus covering adequately the transportation costs. Liturgical furniture of a good standard is also produced; also some inspired wood-carved figures and intricately decorated wooden door surrounds. All this has "Western" potential, but needs western confidence and people with patience, an understanding of Indian business economy and practice, and persistent marketing skills to be able to get anywhere with it. In the evening I accompanied Aaron to Bishop Trinity's home, where he and his wife made me most welcome. A visit was made to the hostel situated above Bishop Trinity's home, where I was introduced to the staff and to the girls, aged between five and eighteen. The girls living there were from different backgrounds; some were the daughters of sex-workers, others were of tribal background from the villages in the mountains around Vellore. Living in the hostel gave them the chance for better schooling, and of course such educational opportunity meant better future prospects for girls who would otherwise have had little cause for optimism. We exchanged songs, and Aaron and I left amidst the sound of loud bangs as yet more Divali crackers blitzed our ears.

We drove out towards Karigiri, to visit Dr.R.Chanrasekhar at the new Navjeevan Asha Centre in Sevoor. A two-day conference there was coming to an end, and I was privileged to join them at the end of proceedings and to hear of some of the sterling work that is being performed by various

Christian agencies amongst young people in India. I was particularly interested to meet Mr S.Sweeharan from Delhi, who was part of a team involved in AIDS awareness work and clinical outreach.

The speciality of the Navjeevan Asha Centre in Sevoor was to turn around the lives of boys with behavioural or severe educational problems, and to rescue street children. It was a wonderful experience to visit the hostel after meeting the conference delegates. A startlingly noisy welcome was give to me in song and on the drums. A disciplined but extravert presentation was given in voice and song. Two of the boys gave moving testimonies, similar to the ones printed above, as to how the Centre and Christ had changed their lives from being street-kids to responsible young adults. Afterwards they permitted me to teach them some western songs, and I was then feted with what was becoming a little too familiar that day – food! But how generous people are here, giving everything possible, including close, caring friendship.

I returned to Karigiri quite late, full of Indian hospitality, but also thankful for the spiritual nourishment I had received that day. I felt humbled by the strength of efforts being made by Indian Christians to serve Christ with fullest commitment. It makes our English efforts look very tame – we have much to learn.

On the Hindu feast of Divali I awoke in the stillness of Karigiri to hear in the distance the sound of firecrackers firing on all cylinders (and that at six in the morning!). The sound didn't cease the whole day, and there were remnants of Divali revelry for the whole of my stay in Vellore. We visited St.John's Church in the afternoon, and were given gracious hospitality by Pastor Wilfred. The situation at St.John's must be unique. It is a part of the CSI, but at the same time seems to enjoy a certain independence from it. Worship there is conducted in English, and membership is mainly from the CMC or other health-related centres in Vellore.

Lydia, Paul and Anita very kindly took me out for a special Divali meal in a rather "posh" restaurant, after which we returned to Katpadi to get ourselves ready for an evening trip out into the country. I went off with Lydia and her family to join her in-laws for a Divali get-together. On the way we stopped in central Vellore at the Delhi Confectioners, where we were allowed to sample some delicious sweetmeats. I really thought I had found my career opportunity, but reluctantly left this little slice of heaven on earth, clutching a box of Divali goodies to take with me for the family. We passed through many villages, where people were busy letting off fireworks, particularly some rather dangerous-looking crackers, which are not for the faint-hearted. We arrived at what I thought was our destination, being met in the dark by some of the family with torches. We then proceeded to walk past a deep well, through a banana plantation, through a field of sugar cane, through a fairly shallow river (warm water, thankfully), through someone else's farm and through their bullocks, along a path a foot wide for a few fields, then finally we arrived at the family's farmhouse.

Ramesh's family were extremely welcoming. They spoke no English, and I speak no Tamil. The Revd.Christopher and Paul very kindly engaged me in conversation; and the odd bit of sign language, and the sharing of visual humour kept us going. The family table groaned with generosity, and a tasty feast was presented for us. Afterwards presents were exchanged, including presents for me. All through the proceedings Sheryl had been in her element, and even became brave enough to chase the dog around the veranda – she was definitely getting the better of him!

On the previous Tuesday Lydia kindly offered to buy me a Dhoti (an Indian Sarong). I procrastinated, but then having been persuaded that such a garment would gain me much respect, decided to give it a go. Thursday was the day when I plucked up the courage to wear it. So it was off to The Fort and the Temple with Silas that morning, with bemused onlookers trying to figure out who this weird pink guy was dressed as an Indian gent! As it happened, it seemed to be appreciated by those who came up to speak to me (and that was quite a few that day), and I was paid the compliment by Silas of being "70% Indian" (but just a pity about my blue eyes and pink skin!).

The main visit on the Thursday was to the impressive Ruhsa Hospital, which as a Christian Foundation was providing essential hospital care to a large rural area outside of Vellore at affordable rates. Additionally there was the provision of care for those suffering from polio, and an impressive School of Nursing for some eighty young women from rural and deprived areas, for whom such training was put within their financial and educational reach, for their benefit and that of those whom they would in future serve.... It is obvious that American missionary vision of the last century (particularly that of Dr.Ida Scudder) has provided Vellore and the surrounding region with medical care that is second to none in the Indian sub-continent. But what is even more commendable is what the Christians of Vellore are doing NOW in the field of health, community and vocational projects.

First thing on the next morning Bishop Trinity and I joined The Revd.Christopher and The Revd.Aaron in the blessing of land for the building of a Care Home for Convalescents and for Foreign Visitors I then took "Donald" and an assortment of puppets into the Nursery school attached to Katpadi Church. Donald, with his shock of red hair, was a bit too much for one or two of the youngsters, but was greeted with exuberance by most of the others, particularly Sheryl!

Aaron then whisked me off to the excellent Kasam Agricultural Institute. Mr Samuel Sankar, the director, was rightly proud of the research achievement of the institute, and was doing some good work in encouraging sensible organic practices amongst the ordinary farming community to its obvious benefit. The aims of the Agricultural Institute were an echo of Ruhsa, with a lot of worthwhile effort being put into the empowerment of the disadvantaged and particularly of women. In the afternoon we were able to spend a little time at Vandavasi Hospital, with some excellent and extremely affordable courses offered to young men and women in the field of electronics, air-conditioning engineering, motor mechanical engineering and the like - and with enthusiastic students to match. The young people come from villages within reasonable bus distance, and have only to find 1,500/- for fees. It was quite obvious that these fees do little to cover the real costs of the course, and this is putting a strain on the hospital's resources, but it is seen as vital work nevertheless.

On the Saturday, after a tour around the CMC Hospital in Vellore with Mythili, and having the pleasure of meeting her father and mother; I was then introduced to the Chaplaincy Department, and met the Head of Department, The Revd Immanuel, also an assistant chaplain, The Revd.Prema. Because of the far-reaching catchment of the hospital (all India, and many countries beyond), services on a Sunday in the Chapel have to be conducted in nine different languages, although not all at once! It is impressive to note that the Hospital Chapel is at the centre of the hospital, and is a recognition that Christ is at the centre of all that is done in this excellent hospital. Later that afternoon Silas and I went to the Anbuillam School and Rehabilitation Centre for Cerebral Palsied children.

On the Sunday a recovered John accompanied me the whole day on a liturgical feast with the Revd Jacob Vivek. Morning worship was at Bishop Rufus's favourite church, Redeemer Church at Sathuvachari.

Preparing to be a Guest

Whether staying in someone's home, in a guest house or hotel it is very helpful to prepare and particularly useful to find out about local customs.

Guests should fight against shyness when they first arrive in a home in a new culture and perhaps country. Guests should ask about things in the host's way of life which they do not understand.

Photographs: Barbara Butter

It is unlikely that the host's culture will be similar to that of the guest

Many African families are used to communal living

Sometimes a little self-help is needed

All cultures differ and it is unlikely that the host's culture will be similar to that of the guest. It would be disappointing if cultures were similar as there would be little to learn. It is vital for guests to be open-minded and flexible, even if this is a struggle, when they find that there are different ways of doing things, including domestic organisation, times of eating, ways of eating and of course the food itself. If something is new there is almost more reason to try it when it is offered, as part of the learning experience of the visit. The exception to this will be when there is a health or religious taboo, which hosts will understand. People who visit the developing world from the west must find ways of sharing their food needs and their need to drink boiled water with their hosts.

If guests are coming from another country to Britain they should be aware that life in Britain is very expensive. It may not be helpful for guests to make long-distance telephone calls unless they check very carefully with hosts. It may be much easier for some guests to ask for help in sending a fax or e-mail to family and friends in another country.

If guests have travelled by air to their destination they should be informed about the rules of air travel, and should not carry excess baggage, but rather weigh everything carefully to check that it is within the correct limits before they go to the airport at the end of the visit.

Preparing to be a host

It is important to remember that guests may be entirely new to the culture of their hosts and that things which may seem obvious to hosts may be far from obvious to guests and may need careful explanation. It is important that hosts give time to talking to their guests about everyday living. It is important for hosts, in any country or culture, to help guests to feel at home early in the visit, to share their way of life but not to ask any unnecessary questions, especially personal questions, of the guest.

It is a good idea to offer a guest a simple map of the house, and of the area he/she is living in. It is helpful to provide information about buses and trains, and about the underground service if there is one. A sketch or local map would be very helpful, showing how to reach shops, parks and places of interest. The best way to orientate someone is to walk around the area with them. Guests will not find it easy to remember any details if they are driven around.

It is helpful to check with guests about whether he/she has any special needs for diet, hygiene or culture. This could be done before the guest arrives. The needs could be religious. The different religions often have dietary rules, and sometimes they have prescribed ways of washing. Muslims for example must bathe in running water and not in still water. It is very important for hosts to be direct and to ask guests about special needs, because otherwise it may be assumed by guests that their needs are well known and therefore need no explanation.

A good host will be sensitive to the comfort of a guest. What may be an acceptable indoor temperature to a host may cause a guest to shiver, especially if he/she has just arrived from a much hotter climate. It is particularly important to check the temperature in a guest's room. It will also be helpful if the host checks whether the guest has adequate clothing and equipment for the visit.

Being a host and being a guest is a reciprocal joy. No one is wholly giving or wholly receiving, and the fun is doubled if hosts and guests are open-minded and generous towards each other.

The travel guidebook scene is changing fast

Extra notes for Families Receiving Guests

"Everything is so different here. People are in a hurry. How do I ask? How do I find the way? So many cars – People don't smile."

Guests need some time to rest. Do not make their programmes too full. Visiting can be tiring especially struggling with a strange language. A simple programme, however, is helpful – so that people know what to expect and where the next meal is coming from.

Many Africans are used to communal living – they will walk from one room to another and move around the kitchen or garden without being asked. They do not feel the need to be 'given permission' to wander about. This makes hospitality easier. There is no constraint about staying put, as with English visitors. Sharing cooking and other jobs is normal.

The sun shines more in other countries. Do we make up for it with cheerfulness? It's a long way from home and can be lonely.

Family is very important. People will always want to tell you about their children. Have they any photographs?

Schooling is also very important. Is it difficult? Are there problems with paying for it?

Books cost money – but heavy luggage and heavy presents can be very expensive to take home. BEWARE OF EXCESS BAGGAGE.

Motherhood is very important. Ask if their spouse is at home with-the family while your visitor is away in this country.

How will she/he manage? Do they have enough to live on – especially if the wage earner is away? Are any of the children at home, sick? Do they have handicaps?

Shared meals are very important. Do they eat from a family dish? How is the food prepared? What are their favourite foods? What dishes do they have for a celebration? Do they eat with the right hand?

Choosing Guidebooks

The travel guidebook scene is changing fast. Some feel it may not be long before we prepare for our journeys through donning virtual reality-type headsets to "pre-visit" certain destinations to help us choose between options. Then we will actually tour the globe with hand-held wands with a/v facilities. Soon the traditional guidebook may become a museum piece.

Perhaps, but somewhat like the development of art after the invention of photography, paper-based, cheaply-produced, but readily up datable tourist guidebooks will be more likely to take on new forms complementing the growing range of cybernetic aids to travel. Indeed, there are signs this is already starting. Go into any good bookshop with a decent travel section and we may find a growing range of attractive paper-based products on the shelves. These are usually fairly easy to stuff into a travel bag or rucksack and although they may get travel stained and dog eared in use, they do not risk the technical malfunctions of their cybernetic competitors. They can also be annotated as and when required, and passed on afterwards to other global adventurers.

However, the circumstances for travel to and within almost all destinations, are changing rapidly, and it is a hard job for guidebook publishers and their keen competitors to keep up. Because of this, it is often unwise to recommend particular titles, authors and publishers, for guidebooks to specific countries. Rather, it is arguably much better for travellers who want to prepare properly to spend some time browsing in a really good travel bookshop, looking at the range of titles on offer for the places they want to visit. If, in so doing, they heed the criteria which follow, they will end up not only educating themselves in the process, and further perfecting their consumer critique, but also helping to send a message to authors, publishers and book shops. The message is to maintain a high standard of products that will encourage and inform still more people to an attitude of enjoyable, responsible and responsive travel.

Firstly, to pick up an earlier point, a guidebook must be fairly portable, and reasonably durable. It must also be sensibly priced. This, of course, leads into the more basic consumer question of whether you really get value for money (and this, these days, applies to tourism as well as so much else.) Good illustrations in a guidebook are important, though avoid the kind of "glossy guides" strong on visuals but weak on content. Bear in mind also the vast shanty town or concrete beach strip developments that may lie just out of the frame of some of the best photographs. Who said the camera never lies ?

Secondly, look carefully at the title page details (publisher, title, date of edition) and the level of the author's biographical credentials. How well do the writers really know the country/areas concerned? Check the contents page layout, approach and content and see if there is a good index at the back. Any good guidebook must contain accurate travel, visa, currency, medical and hotel etc. information, and details of where to obtain the very latest updates on these, and other essentials, where especially rapid changes may occur. There should be decent general maps, and main town plans, and details of where to get hold of more up-to-date maps and further reading listed in a good bibliography. There should be clear, current information on what to do, and who to contact, in various kinds of medical, financial, political or other emergencies. A good note on the language(s), and sets of essential phrases for greetings, a range of activities and use in emergencies should be included.

Thirdly, the guidebook should have a good, but not too "heavy" introduction to the geography, history, religion(s), customs and current circumstances of the country/region/area: preferably these should be written by a knowledgeable local person, or by an author who has excellent local knowledge and contacts. There should be a good section on local customs and traditions and what is expected of the tourist as a good "guest"(greetings, manners, taboos, bargaining, tipping, giving alms, photos). There should also be a clear progression from these introductory sections into chapters highlighting the main themes, places, peoples and activities of interest in the country, both from the foreigner's and resident's points of view. Every tourist's – and resident's – background, tastes and interests are different, but visitors seeking better to relate to people, places and cultures in the places that they visit have somehow to live the tension implied in GK Chesterton's observation viz., *the tourist comes to see what (s)he wants to see: the visitor comes to see what is there".*

Items like food and eating out, clothes, shopping, accommodation and – yes! information on sanitation are very important to many, if not most travellers. They should be well covered in the guidebook.

A good guide will suggest – either more or less explicitly – ways and means of experiencing the scenery, life and culture of a destination area which are a real fun learning experience, offering the pleasant delights that often come in surprising places and encounters with the people. Definite "no go" areas or activities should be clearly identified in the text! Even seasoned travellers will make cultural "mistakes" from time to time, mainly unwittingly, but experience for them usually brings a certain attitude of foresight and sensitivity. The author(s) of a good guidebook should show this.

It is wise to compare several guidebooks on the same country or region which are on the shelf in the travelshop. No doubt we will have recommendations from friends from time to time: look out for such titles, or their updates, and compare and contrast. If time is short, a quick skim of the shelf is helpful first time round, with a few hurried notes of some attractive titles which can be browsed through more carefully on a return visit, before a final choice for purchase is made. In some cases, if interest, desires, and money affords, it may be worth getting two, or even three good guidebooks on a destination especially if they clearly complement one another. If you are travelling with a group, and in particular, if you are a group leader, this may sometimes be a good idea: such books can be shared by the group.

Please also refer to our book list at the end of the book

Tour Guides

It can be very helpful to discover a tour guide once you are in the country of your choice. A good guide can make your visit much more valuable even it is only for day's outing. Choose a guide who seems to be open to suggestions from you and can offer you plenty of options. Before setting off be sure to let your guide know your needs and hopes.

Be sure to ask for maps of the area you hope to visit and for any other leaflets. Be clear about times of departure and return, and also the price. All this should be done before the departure.

If you suffer from travel sickness let your guide know. You may need lots of loo stops, or stops for refreshments. You may have other needs, be sure to say what they are so that your guide can be aware of them.

If you are particularly interested in birds, plants, architecture, views or perhaps a short walk, then let your guide know in advance, it will all help to make the tour more interesting and satisfying for all.

If you have enjoyed the day you may wish to thank your guide in some way, go prepared.

Being There

Chapter Three

Being There

'Go placidly amid the noise and the haste and remember what peace there may be in silence".
Desiderata. Max Ehrmann

Travellers will only manage to get inside the culture they are visiting and hoping to learn from if they are able to live day by day, focusing on each moment as it comes. It may not be helpful to think too much about home and about contrasts between cultures, for good or bad, though who decides what is good or bad is a difficult if not impossible question to answer. It may not be helpful to think ahead too much either, because then the present, with its interests and also its boredoms, will be lost.

Watching. Adapting

It is invaluable if visitors to new cultures are able to give up something of the normal control they have over their lives and thus to allow the hosts to take over without being overcome by feelings of powerlessness. These feelings may be particularly strong in professional people who are used to being in charge of their lives and of most of the situations they are involved in. Many visitors may find it especially hard to depend on their hosts when they are staying with a family, and may have to learn to respond to suggestions instead of initiating them. It is only in this way that it is at all possible to stand in the shoes of the host, to see through the eyes of the host and to understand why people in the host community do the things they do.

This ability to understand the new culture has a far greater value than the simple experience and insight gained. The insights may be shared with others so that a wider understanding of people and their cultural differences may grow. This may lead to greater tolerance and even reconciliation in difficult situations.

Accepting Hospitality

Please also see the section on "Being a Guest" for help in living creatively with hosts.

How hospitality will be accepted should be thought about before a visit takes place. There may be slight differences in approach, depending on the arrangements made before the visit. Whatever practical arrangements are made it is vital for the guest who wishes to experience another way of life to fleetingly forget his or her own way of doing things, or at least to be able to recognise that their way is not the only way, and to accept the new way and to be able to recognise its value. For example, a visitor who comes from a culture where she prefers to be alone and to read for much of the time, will not learn very much if she pursues her normal lifestyle in the middle of an African village, where the extended family lives together and shares practical work like gardening. A visitor who pursues her own ways may find herself the centre of a very concerned community.

Staying in a Hotel or Guest House

It is helpful to stay in a place where local people also stay so that you can meet them and learn at meal and leisure times. The local guests may introduce you to people in the wider community. The local church may also be able to help.

Witnessing a new way of Christian Baptisms in Bangladesh

*Meeting People
of many
World faiths*

Meeting People of Many World Faiths

There may be particular insights associated with inter-faith visits and exchanges. As in all visits, sensitivity and listening are vital. Always find out as much as you can about the faiths whose members you may be meeting before you set off. There are many excellent books available. Christians Aware has published some books on meeting people of other faiths and can also advise.

You may also be able to meet people of the faiths you are learning about in your own country and even sometimes in your own school, place of work or local area. This may have many advantages, including the opportunity to be introduced to friends and members of families in the country you are going to. This can also of course work the other way round. You may meet people on your travels who will offer introductions to their friends and families in your home country. A London school teacher who went to Mauritius met many people of the Hindu, Muslim and Buddhist faiths whilst she was there, as well as meeting the people of her own Christian faith who were her hosts. When she returned to London she was able to meet relatives of the people of all the faiths she had met in Mauritius and to visit their homes, faith communities and places of worship. She also found that there were actually children in her school who had members of the family in Mauritius. She had been totally unaware of this and of the faiths of the children.

It is sometimes a wise choice for some people to meet members of other faiths in a new situation and country first of all. This is likely lead to confidence and understanding, which will make it easier for encounters to take place in the local community at home.

Sometimes meeting people of other faiths in a different country from your own can be very inspiring, and can encourage a deeper commitment to your own faith on your return home. Two people who went to Chennai, (Madras) in South India were fortunate to be there at the time of the consecration of the Sri Ramakrishna Temple in Myalpore. The ceremony was attended by more and 30,000 people from all over India. On the day set aside for work for religious harmony, members of the Hindu, Jain, Buddhist, Sikh, Christian and Muslim faiths gave presentations on their faith perspectives and on ways forward to a peaceful and tolerant India, where all could live together and accept each other. One member of the group wrote, "This made us think about our role as Christians, representing Christians Aware and also our home communities. What could we do to further the vision. We have so much to learn about human values, compassion, tolerance, helping those less fortunate than ourselves, self-sufficiency and acceptance of our fellow human beings."

Mark Coleman has written about his experiences in visiting people of other faiths in Calcutta and Cape Town.

'When I was at school I had to write an essay in French class entitled "Les voyages forment la jeunesse" – travel shapes youth. I agreed with the proposition. I think I got a good mark !

My experiences of overseas travel and encounter with people of other countries, races and cultures has been a very powerful influence on me. More inspiring, than the expensive education at school and university, it has given me a direction and a vocation and helped me relate to and learn from people of other races and cultures in this country. Without Calcutta, would I have gone to Sheffield? Without Cape Town, would have I chosen the job in Liverpool ? Perhaps not !

I have a theory about travel, identity and transformation. We live between the two poles of identity (who we are) and transformation (who we could be.) Without our identity, without knowing who we each are, we are nowhere at all. Without transformation we are stuck, and the new life of God – where justice and peace flourish – is a long way away.

Travelling to Calcutta with Christians Aware in 1983 helped me get a better sense of who I was and who I could become. I had to tell my stories to people who made no assumptions, or ones different from mine. I had to explain myself. But most excitingly by discovering other people of other faiths,and hearing their stories I began to see both what we share and what we have that is diverse and different. Either way, this was for me a sense of God's great ingenuity with people. Overall I learned, and was inspired.

Travel has indeed shaped and formed me. Names and faces are there in my personal story books – like my own communion of saints – Shourabh, Shanti, Nellie, John, Elizabeth, Marie, Daniel to name but a few. They shared their stories of oppression overcome and faith passionately held. To the privilege of those encounters I have tried to respond ever since .

On trip to South Africa in October 2001 a Canon of the Cathedral, Chris Chivers said at Friday prayers at a mosque that "insularity has failed" and that "those who sit round a table are less likely to look down the barrel of a gun". We should not forget that our international friendships are real and vital peace work. There is nothing more important than that. Small relationships, are holy and precious things.

The mosque was packed. Because of the September 11th world event, Friday prayers at the Claremont Main Road Mosque took the form of an Interfaith Peace Service. A quiet looking place, looking from the outside like a Protestant chapel, the mosque it is in one of the busiest and wealthiest shopping and residential districts of Cape Town. Women and men and a mix of races, members of parliament and people of different faiths all gathered under the auspices of the Cape Town Interfaith Initiative to reflect in the context of prayer on the September 11 2001 atrocity in the United States and responses made to it.

In his welcome a Muslim leader, Fahmi Gamielden, spoke of the Muslim community being horrified at the abominable acts, but was equally dismayed at the bombing of children in the name of retribution and justice. The world is far more complex than is being portrayed, he said. Islam and other world religions are against violence in whatever form it manifests itself. He recalled that Mohammed hosted Christians at Medina, debating issues of mutual concern. In the darkest days of apartheid Muslims and Christians sustained each others spiritual needs. At this service, to be seen against this background – a humble effort was made to be with friends of other faiths. Fahmi concluded the service by saying, "We pray to God to accept our sincere efforts and to establish peace and justice in the world."

In his address the Revd Chris Chivers, Canon Precentor of Cape Town Anglican Cathedral, brought a 'message of peace'. He spoke of a moving scene in the film 'Gandhi', where the Mahatma joined in the grief of bereaved Muslim parents. The challenge, he said, would be for them to find a Hindu child and to bring that child up as a Hindu. Meeting at a time of suffering and uncertainty that story encapsulates the journey we are now on. The reality is that the world is deeply divided between rich and poor, and in attitudes to human rights. The faiths we embrace are often the cause of shifting blocks and alliances. Christians have been involved in conflict, the enslavement of Africa, the eradication of civilisations, and the ransacking of Muslim lands. Millions of Jews have been subjected to anti-Semitism. Millions of fellow Africans in South Africa have suffered because of those doing God's work. His followers have too often ignored his pathways of peace, love and compassion.

Chris Chivers said that he sees his task to be enabling Christians to be better Christians. "I have been made a better Christian," he said, "not least by eating meals and having the friendship and support of people of other faiths."

Staying with a family in Croatia

Appreciation of the place, the people and their work

The value of simply being in a new place and learning from a new culture comes out from these extracts from travellers' diaries.

Staying with a Family

On Christians Aware visits the visitors often go to stay with a family in the host community for between a few days and a week. The family visits normally take place either in the middle of the programme or at the end, so that the visitor has already had some experience of the local culture.

Members of a group often begin to feel a little apprehensive as the time for the family visit approaches. They have usually adjusted to being part of a group and now have to change again, and be alone in a family and community. It is helpful if the group can talk about theses feelings before the visits take place.

It is usually both helpful and challenging to remind members that if they had wanted a " home away from home" they might as well have stayed at home.

A discussion on what it means to be pilgrim may be useful at this point, so that members leave for the family visits with a genuine desire to learn, to be sensitive and to listen before talking.

Members may be challenged to " see through new eyes," the eyes of the family they are visiting, for only in this way will they appreciate the richness of the culture they are fleetingly part of.

A reminder about different views of time may be helpful, because sometimes on family visits people do have to wait around for long periods, and some find this very difficult. Time can also be a problem the other way round, when hosts are good timekeepers, and guests are slow to prepare themselves for events.

Visitors to Barbados wrote:

'Stained archways through to the stairs, kitchen and bathroom. There is a little garden at the back. Most of the homes are bungalows. There is no need for glass in the windows. Shutters keep out the weather and allow the breeze to blow through the house, keeping everything beautifully cool. Many American programmes are shown on television. I was surprised how much British news is of interest. On Sunday morning we got up really early for Church. The church was packed and everyone looked very smart in their Easter clothes, the women in white or cream dresses and wearing very elegant high heeled shoes and the little girls with their hair plaited into elaborate styles. Muriel had been up for hours before me preparing lunch; spiced roast port, salads, rice with peas, sweet potatoes with pineapple and lots more. I find it hard to sleep at night. There are different noises from the ones I am used to; music, mostly reggae, dogs barking and cockerels crowing. Just about everyone seems to keep chickens.'

"… We went to their home in St.James. What a lovely house they have right on the beach. On Sunday we were up at 4.00 a.m. to attend the 5.00 a.m. Easter morning service. After breakfast the eldest son, Martin took me out in his boat, after lunch we went to the kite flying at the garrison…"

"… I waited nervously on Friday evening for a car to arrive to whisk me away to I knew not what. I wasn't prepared for what I saw when I walked into the house. There were a lot of young boys running around; to add to my confusion there was Judy the housekeeper and Judy who helped Mrs.Mayers in her hairdressing salon downstairs. Finally there was a lodger. I retired early on Friday evening to my own apartment, a life of luxury. We spent Saturday shopping and driving and in the evening we went to the pepperpot, a night-club owned by Eddy Grant. Believe it or not I managed to get up for Church. I had been forewarned that I would have to stand up and speak about Christians Aware. Sunday lunch was the traditional Bajan fare of rice'n peas, salad, chicken and macaroni cheese. Sophia and her mother whisked me away after lunch laden with fresh pineapple and apples….."

First, I remember the heat and the warmth of the people. It was so hot especially in St.Christopher's school, that you could only do one thing at a time and then have a rest. I have never spent so much time under a cold shower or in the sea! Yet there was so much friendliness and so many new experiences, plus the beauty of the Island that one didn't really mind.

Secondly, I remember the worship. In some ways it took me back to my childhood, so very Anglican, but with a unique Caribbean flavour. I enjoyed the vitality of the singing and the enthusiasm at the heart of the worship. I do hope that the young people will continue to be involved in the life of the church – certainly a lot of concern was expressed at a meeting with the Friendship Youth Group.

Thirdly, I remember our meeting with the Dean and a fascinating chat with him on the walk to our aeroplane at the end of our stay. I was particularly interested in his love of Anglican liturgy and music, and in the remarkable way he related the Gospel to both the culture and the political situation in Barbados. All this has somehow niggled around my mind alongside an interesting reflection from the Cuban General Secretary of the Caribbean Conference of Churches, based on the island. During his stay in Barbados he told us that he had attended a local Anglican church where he found the preaching and the application of the Gospel to be excellent, in some contrast to the worship. He found the very reverse in some of the free Churches, (with a Pentecostal flavour!) where the worship was livelier but the preaching and witness much weaker.

Fourthly, I remember our time with the Caribbean Conference of Churches, and its mandate;

> Promoting Ecumenism and Social Change
> In obedience to Jesus Christ and in solidarity with the poor.

I was impressed by the people-centred self-help community development programmes and projects, based on needs which the communities themselves identify. It reminded me once again how truly liberating it is to be and to work within ecumenical environments.

A visitor to Mauritius wrote:

"…As Roman Catholics we attended the parish church of Notre Dame de Lourdes in Rose Hill…at lunch time relatives and friends came with Easter greetings and the whole family congregated for a celebratory lunch. As on the Saturday we spent the afternoon visiting some of the beauty spots on the island. On Easter Monday there were hundreds of families camping on the edge of the beach. There were games among the trees, people swimming and children playing in the lovely clear blue sea, and all the fun and enjoyment was accompanied by groups singing to the sound of guitars and the drums on which they play the music for their traditional Sega dance. I think my friends and I were the only non-Creoles on the beach…."

A visitor to Kenya wrote:

"…On the evening when I arrived I met two evangelists, Samuel and David. Next morning Samuel, Mary and David met me at about nine o'clock and I walked with them round the parish visiting the church members. We looked first at the tea-buying centre where the local growers bring their tea to sell. We then had a glass of tea at the chai bar. We visited the home of a local teacher, which was very well built. I met Samuel's brother and aunt. His aunt was digging up sweet potatoes and she gave me one to try. In the evening the family, a friend and I were invited to have dinner at the home of the

Visiting an extended Maasai family in North-Western Kenya

81

local tribal chief.. I attended a service of morning prayer … and gave a short talk and afterwards I had lunch with the church elders….we had corn on the cob, arrowroot, irio, sweet potatoes and banana. On my return to the vicarage I went to the church..and talked to the local KAYO (Kenya Anglican Youth Organisation) group….later I shared presents with the family….Eliazar gave me a cowrie shell from Mombassa. He said that visiting Mombassa had been like going to a foreign country. I went to Kagongo in three matatus (Kenya taxis), we stopped at a friend's house and they gave me hot milk to drink…"

"...When we arrived they started singing to us, clapping. Inside, over half the church was full of children; then the adults came. The service lasted two and a half hours. They had two sermons…we went outside; Peter told us we were going to have dinner at the house of the child who was baptised. We turned off the road into a small passageway, with large hedges on either side. Small children ran around staring at us; eventually we got to the house…I couldn't help noticing the kitchen; it was made of corrugated iron, and bits of material and other bits and pieces. I could see about six small children eating from enamel plates….We went inside and we met the father of the house; his wife came in carrying a pot and a kettle of hot water. She came round and washed our hands ...the chapatis were delicious, but, as I think we all discovered, in Kenya the meat is very tough…We went to the house Peter is building. It is made of wood and has a corrugated iron roof. He is making money by making dried flower pictures, by sticking the flowers onto wood. He gave us one … we went next door…it was tiny inside, the lady made us a cup of tea. She boiled the tea with the milk and sugar in …"

Kenyan and Bajan visitors to England wrote:

"We came from Kenya and Barbados to stay in Wombwell near Barnsley… The places of interest were the Methodist Churches, the countryside and the coal pits….a number of people are using coal in their houses to keep warm… though some of the coal pits have been closed and many people have lost their jobs…we visited three of the five Methodist churches…there are lots of activities to bring people together…"

A visitor to India wrote:

"…I was standing alongside Shanti's bed on the veranda of his house in Orissa... It was 6.30 am. We greeted each other and then I washed and we shared a meal. I was so relieved to see him and to discuss my journey, including Christmas night when I had taken a bus from Calcutta to his village.. On my first afternoon in Orissa I went with Shanti's brother and a friend to one of the tribal schools eight miles away. We took push bikes along the dusty roads, crossed rivers and cycled through paddy fields…"

Eight weeks on, and caught up in the flurry of parish work, our Christians Aware trip to Barbados seems to have been in another life! But as I sit reflecting, I remember everyone in our party, the people we met and the event we shared with great affection.

Work Camps

Work-camps are not always easy to arrange by a host community, but when they are possible they are an excellent way, through hard and happy times, of giving participants of many backgrounds the opportunity to share a common goal and to develop mutual understanding and friendship. Alf Chipman, who joined with Christians aware in many Kenyan work-camps, said, " Work-camps are always hustle and bustle… just the sheer magnitude of doing in 8 or 9 days what ought to take the same group a full month, means we must press on continually…the hustles and bustles are always different…they rub off the sharp corners and they reveal our weak points…."

Work Camps

Photographs: Barbara Butler

83

A Work Camp in Kenya

"Blisters and aching arms, picks, axes and shovels, mattocks and crowbars, thirst and tiredness, basking in sunshine – these are probably the immediate recollections of many who took part in the work-camp at Naro Moru. The aim was to dig foundations for a two storey block, so that the youth centre could be used for residential groups… in all there were about 35 of us working, Kenyans and British…we were split into 4 mixed groups, each allocated to dig a different side… shock number one came within a minute – the ground was so dry it seemed like a rock – how could we ever dig in this soil? Shock number two closely followed, we were told that all the foundations had to be 4 feet deep and not less than 22 inches wide… by end of the day the first blisters had been created and had burst… but a start had been made…. Each day 5 or 6 people were relieved of digging duties and dispatched to assist in the kitchen… although the hours were longer the pace of work was far more relaxed… towards the end of the final day; miraculously the foundations for all four corners of the building had been dug…then a huge lorry arrived laden with weighty stone slabs…and yes, the slabs could wait for another day, and another group…."

The Christians Aware Work Camps in Tanzania

"The tall peak of the Mount was like a silent sentinel, observing our arrival at the small village of Lewa. The beautiful green Peak, symbolised the fertility of this area . It captivated us.

As so often in our tour, we were becoming accustomed to the magnificent scenery that surrounded us: breathtaking views and amazing alterations in a Chameleon landscape. The parish of Lewa was no exception. The wonderful Choral welcome of our hosts was no anomaly, either. This was to herald the start of a firm friendship, developing through the mutual objective of helping to complete the programmed work camp.

The second of the work camps organised, was probably the most enjoyable, and satisfying. We were able to finish beyond all expectations the task that lay ahead of us.

The first project was to dig the foundations for the new church at Mgombezi, and had obviously been chosen as the "breaking in" session in which " … soft white hands were soon decorated in a numerous variety of coloured blisters, and caused many people much discomfort." Nevertheless, the courage of the 'workers' shone through, and despite the painful palms and aching muscles, (that had obviously gone soft in the embrace of our favoured arm chair back home), we preserved and succeeded in starting the project. (It is hoped that this will provide the necessary stimulus for the local parishioners to continue our good work).

While we were there, we could not help acknowledge the relentless energy of the local people who aided us with the digging. Their example provided us with constant incentive to keep going… The Africans seemed unperturbed and seemed to be capable of working all day, even some of the small children, barefooted, swung hoes and spades with incredible energy and strength.

The experience at Mgombezi seemed to be upstaged by the Lewa project. It encapsulated the whole trip, in terms of the working and learning philosophies gained from each other. Despite, the obvious language difficulty – Swahili is not exactly part of the national curriculum, we struck up a firm working rapport, and were indeed, privileged to enjoy the superb hospitality of our generous hosts.

The project at Lewa was primarily organised through the development Department of the Diocese, under the co-ordination of Joseph Ngerza and Stephen Riley. Stephen took over the responsibility of the Lewa scheme after the tragic death of the predecessor. The incident had caused the project to lose all momentum, for almost a year, until Stephen was appointed the job of putting it back on its feet.

Primarily the project is part of a development initiative designed at helping villages through a process of "Pull yourself up by your own bootstraps philosophy". Conceived as part of a nutrition programme, the project aimed to provide a large fish pond in which to grow the fast growing and nutritious fish called Tilapia. Fortunately, the majority of the pond had been dug when we arrived. Consequently, we were spared a lot of " back- breaking" work, or so we thought. All that remained was to construct the water channel connecting the water source, a fast flowing river, to the pond - a mere 2500 metres of digging, under the fierce heat of the African sun! Planning and executing the design of this channel proved to be quiet a challenge, physically and mentally. Conflicting opinions were derived from a variety of sources. Governmental planners suggested one route for the channel, whilst the development workers and CA group suggested another. The Kenyans and Tanzanians could not always agree on certain technical and management difficulties. All we could do was stand back and let the stream of Swahili pass our heads! Despite this, the operations proceeded extremely well and despite minor set backs we exceeded all expectations and finished the work in barely two days. All that remained was the ardous job of sitting back, watching the water fill the pond and enjoying the delightful meal prepared by our charitable hosts."

As a postscript to this small report, perhaps the words of E.F. Schumacher can best describe the benefit that working at Lewa and Mgombezi can accomplish. Development does not start with goods; it starts with people and their education, organisation and discipline. Without these three, all resources remain latent, untapped potential. " The best aid to give is intellectual aid, a gift of knowledge. A gift of knowledge is infinitely to a gift of material things."

Maybe the experience that was gained during the whole of the Africa trip can be summarised as a process encapsulating these two quotations. In this respect it was not just the CA group that was giving knowledge. It was a vital part of the experience that we were there to learn, just as much to give. Perhaps a final word from Schumacher can illustrate the fundamental concept of the Christians Aware visit to Africa. " The beginning of wisdom is the admission of one's own lack of knowledge"

'WellCome' to Shamburai

"We arrived in Shamburai, having negotiated the rutted road from Arusha, on a sunny Saturday afternoon in September to be greeted by a mass turn out of surrounding villages, not for us but for the market which seemed to cover every square inch of a large patch of waste land in the centre of the village with a wide variety of local produce and artifacts.

On the Sunday Christian worship was much in evidence with three churches on the edge of the village (near where the site for the new well had already been earmarked) either built or nearing completion – Lutheran, a relic of German West Africa, Pentecostal, an American import, and the ubiquitous Roman Catholic – very simple with planks on breeze blocks for seating and a rough floor which offered any intrepid kneelers a true mortification of the flesh. No Anglican presence as yet, so we were able to be ecumenical in our worship.

Work started in earnest on Monday. The site had been marked, the equipment brought as a result of months of intensive fundraising in England, and a sizable workforce from the village rallied around to help us with extra pushing power. Our only expert was a trained hydrologist who , by regular analysis of the mud from beneath the surface, gave us a running commentary on the nearing presence of water and its quality.

The methods were simple and made few concessions to modern technology. No power drilling equipment here other than the power of human strength! We had a series of long interconnecting poles with a device on the end which served the dual purpose of digging and collecting samples of mud which indicated our progress and the proximity of the valued water. This simple device was surmounted by a crossbar on which we alternately pushed or sat to lend weight to the proceedings. Down it went into the soft earth in a way that proved much easier than expected with very few rocks to impede our passage. Five days' work yielded the first water, rather muddy at first, but, as we delved deeper, increasingly pure so that our hydrologist's brow cleared with signs of growing delight at the success of the venture.

It was a marvellous cooperative venture in which all difference of culture and background were forgotten in the joint venture. Villagers came and went as though by rota, but there was always a hard core of regulars to ensure that the project never ran out of man power, although there were a few moments of near muting when the work force was pushed too hard and all diplomatic skills of our leader had to be brought into play. As the oldest participant, I was hailed as Babu (grandfather) and was the cause of frequent, but good humoured, hilarity, wherever I slipped or fell off the crossbar as I regularly did.

We had to depart before completion for other building activities which involved installing arches in a new church on the outskirts of Arusha, but we did return a week later to see the results of our handiwork, the well complete, a pump installed and fresh water flowing freely down a newly constructed channel.

We were hosted by the village: work done, this was a day for eating, drinking and speech making. Fellow-workers joined us and we were all one again but this time in a mood of joyful celebration rather than hard work. I shall never forget the spirit, warmth and cooperative effort of the villages of Shamburai from whom, in the spirit of Christians Aware, we learned infinitely more than we ever contributed."

Work Camp in Britain

"While at the International Gathering the catering became a major nightmare for me. Each day the menu had to be explained to the cooking team, shopping had to be done and milk and bread had to be ordered…but what fantastic cooks everyone turned out to be as imaginations were fired…although I might have looked harassed and rushed at times I have really enjoyed sorting out the meals and diet for everyone…"

Work in Barbados

"We were invited to work at a Cheshire Centre, a residential centre set up for about 12 physically handicapped children… Some of the children are mobile and others are in wheelchairs…initially they were shy, but some eagerly told us their names and showed us round their bedrooms, day room and classrooms. Like children everywhere they wanted to talk, play and joke…. Some members of our group dug up the scrubland so that seeds could be sown for the centre to grow vegetables…"

India

Jane Webb, a nurse, went out to Calcutta over twenty years ago, saw the need of children with twisted limbs, deformed through polio, and went on to do something about their needs. Her centre helps to set twisted limbs straight….

" The Young Men's Welfare Society…began in 1967…with a small night school…now it has grown and developed…but it still retains the "from the bottom up" approach, trying to involve the people in the communities as the means of social change…their work in the area of health has expanded enormously…they also have a system of small low income loans through which people may begin a business which may raise their families above the poverty line…"

"We travelled south of Cuttack to Rajnagar. There, a SODA (Society of Developmental Action in Orissa) scheme on health hygiene was based here in a cyclone area; from the headquarters it was a 4 hour journey by boat, motorbike and sometimes on foot to reach many of the villages and take the message…"

"Everyone finds the initial tour of the Vellore Hospital both exhausting and overwhelming… you cannot imagine the scene in the outpatient department, constructed for 800 patients a day, which now takes at least 3,000 patients plus their families… Later in the week, two of the group suffering from the usual internal troubles of the visitor to India decided to "go through the system" and it was four hours before they got as far as the doctor…"

Sri Lanka

In the early years of Devasarana, a development community in the center of Sri Lanka, there was heavy emphasis on contemplation and this usually led to an awareness of, and dialogue with, the people in the villages round about, mostly Buddhist. Dialogue has led on to working together… and the centre has become more and more involved in the day to day lives and problems of peasants and workers, including cultivation, trade unions, human rights, racial discrimination. Groups who visit the centre are welcome and always join in the work the community is engaged in. One group built a well in a small village near to Devasarana, with the help of the village people and members of Devasarana.

Ruth Challon visited the Poyston Tea Estate and wrote, "My day on the estate is memorable, with 28 women and 4 children. The women were representative of the many hundreds who work in blazing sun and torrential rain plucking the tender most twigs of the tea bushes, filling the bags they carry on their backs from a band on their foreheads. They showed me the scarring of their fingers. Their hours arc long, their wages minute and the conditions in which they are housed are poor. These women fill both the reproductive and the productive roles, feeding and caring for their children before and after their work in the plantation. – We met in a small Roman Catholic Church on the edge of the estate for three hours and used a painting as a focus for self-expression. Each woman placed a brilliant blue glass bead on the picture whilst sharing a burning wish. Later they placed brightly coloured cutouts of hands to symbolize realities they wanted changing or stopping."

Mauritius

Margaret Stones wrote about her visit, "Our host families were lovely….We were impressed by the work being done amongst the homeless by young people, under the guidance of a Roman Catholic priest. Our group was interested in fair trade so a highlight of the visit was when we went to Craft Aid, where we saw how people, who might otherwise not have been employed, were making cards with pressed flowers, packing sugars and making furniture…..We held conversations with people of other faiths about shared community projects."

Pilgrimages

On any journey of pilgrimage the true pilgrim is never a tourist and much more than just a traveller. She or he is ready to give up normal securities and to take great risks to travel, and thus to be enlightened, changed and challenged. The true pilgrim does not have the security of knowing that he/she is on the right path, but is always open, always questioning, always listening to God and to the people around.

The pilgrim in all the main world faiths traditionally faces new experiences but also worry and uncertainty. He or she is leaving a secure place and perhaps a family and friends, and moving off into

Wilderness weekend in Yorkshire

the unknown. The pilgrim is vulnerable and exposed, with the constant challenge to meet strangers, to share new cultures and perhaps difficult climates and lands. There will always be the new experiences, some good and some bad. There will also be the fears, especially of the unknown and of losing everything which is familiar. Some pilgrims even face the fear of losing their lives.

In our section "A group leader's reflection" Zara Fleming prepared herself physically, mentally and spiritually for a huge challenge in taking a group to Mount Kailash. (Page 26)

It is likely that people were first inspired to become pilgrims by natural landscapes, including forests, seas and mountains. Many indigenous people continue to be filled with awe in their traditional surroundings. The tribal people of India go to the sacred groves or forests. The Australian aborigines are, like many nomadic people, inspired by the landscapes they walk through.

People today continue to be inspired by mountains and natural landscapes. Many people find mental, physical and spiritual challenge and the encouragement to change, on mountains. Others find the same challenges and opportunities when they go to wilderness or desert areas of the world. The wilderness has perhaps always been important for those on a spiritual quest. When a group of people at a Christian Aware conference on Lindisfarne, off the Northumberland coast, were asked to share their special places many of them shared natural and often wild places. A student shared her love of being near the sea and of the animation she felt. Someone else spoke of the inspiration of snow, especially of fresh snow on a normally ugly place.

It is perhaps more unusual for the large cities of the world to be seen as inspirational, except perhaps the capital cities with their beautiful buildings. Ordinary cities are often however stimulating and elevating for the many people who go there for work and to meet the community. People are the huge inspiration of most city places, many of which may be ugly and even unhealthy in themselves. Calcutta is large, ugly and polluted, with huge traffic and noise problems and with unspeakable poverty. Nevertheless, the beauty of Calcutta, which makes many people go there time and time again to be up-lifted, is in the communities of people who support each other and welcome the stranger. In Britain the 'Faith in the City' report which came out in 1986 brought out the strength and inspiration of community life. As people visited the materially disadvantaged areas they became more and more inspired by the courage of the people, so that the places themselves became places they wished to return to, to be encouraged by for their own work elsewhere.

Wherever the place may be and whatever it may be, from a hill to a tree or a mountain, to a stone circle, a wooden hut, a great cathedral or an inner city community centre, the journey to it becomes a pilgrimage because of what happens within the pilgrim. The pilgrim goes to imagine, to pray, to think and to meditate perhaps, or simply to be open to new ideas and directions in life.

Examples of pilgrim places follow.

Adams Peak in Sri Lanka is a fascinating mountain. It can be seen from the sea and the old mariners knew what to look for. Arabic travellers carried its repute all over their world. One of the tales was that merciful God, after he had driven out Adam and Eve from Paradise, assigned to them the next best place: Serendib, Island of happy surprise. You climb the long track from Ratnapura in the west, or more conveniently from Hatton in the East; there are stone steps, but irregular and often steep, you should start climbing depending on your stamina, before midnight. During the season, which is from early December or January till full moon in April, multitudes of pilgrims of all religions master the steps and many sing. Sheds spring up along the route. There is much laughter, full of expectation. Before the top a Japanese Buddhist peace pagoda nestles. The wind is cold there. People huddle together in the cold, awaiting sunrise. Imagine the scene after pilgrims climbed during full moon. It stands in the sky, round and soft-bright. The sun rises. The mountain throws its shadow on its sunlit flank, a triangle turned upside down. Many god's and saints were housed or visited here: ancient deities, Adam of course, the Buddha, St. Thomas the Apostle. They all left their footprint by way of visiting cards. They also deposited them at one and the same spot.

St. David's Cathedral in Pembrokeshire has been an inspiration for pilgrims through the ages. From the early years of David's ministry and mission in the middle years of the sixth century, the site on which the cathedral church of St. Andrew and St. David now stands has attracted pilgrims who came seeking refreshment in the beautiful countryside which edges onto the craggy Pembrokeshire coastline, less than a mile away. The cathedral is the mother church for the diocese of St. David's, the largest in the Anglican province of Wales.

The fact that St. David's still draws thousands of pilgrims within its peaceful walls is itself a witness in our busy world of the continuity of the site's witness to the Christian faith, and, in its earlier centuries to the particular emphasis of spirituality which is now commonly referred to as Celtic Spirituality.

> "The cathedral as it stands today is naturally the product of centuries of adaptation and experiment as the need arose in different ages to accommodate larger numbers of pilgrims and add to the building chapels, transepts and nave which were all to the glory of God. David's original cell would have been in keeping with the sort of simple stone shelters from which the community set about its mission, working in a triangle moving northwards up to Aberacron. These early communities, based along the western coast of the Irish Sea and extending southwards into Cornwall and Brittany, escaped the turmoil which was the formation of England. Roman occupation of Britain was not as extensive to the west as elsewhere and after the Roman legions had left, the pagan Saxon invaders were halted before reaching the Severn. Thus the community life which David and the other Celtic Saints founded, flowered in a way which may not have been possible otherwise. That is not to say that they lived a life cut off from the busy world which they inhabited. Far from it. The communities which flourished along the western coast of Wales were peppered with busy ports and trade was active between Gaul and the Mediterranean lands by western sea routes. It was through this connection with Gaul that the very deep attachment to the monastic ideal and vision became implanted into Welsh Celtic soil."

One person went on a pilgrimage to **Ladakh** in the Himalayas and wrote about her experiences.

> "I chose to go to Ladakh alone. Travelling with a harmonious companion is both pleasant and helpful in times of perplexity, but it can also shield one from personal new experiences. Travelling alone can be exciting, challenging, liberating – giving the imagination free rein so that all that is offered within a new experience can be savoured consciously, with an openness of heart and mind.
>
> At the age of 62, and as a single woman, I travelled to India via British Airways, and landed in one of the hottest and most humid spots – Delhi in July. This was necessary for my purpose, but not recommended if avoidable…. I had a strong inner conviction to make this visit, though I did not know why at the time. I knew but one Indian person in India. And he, bless him, was there at the airport to meet me and rescue me from a barrage of persuasive taxi drivers vying for my custom. Soon afterwards he put me on an internal flight to Leh, Ladakh's capital, and had arranged for me to stay with his parents. A great start to the adventure.

*Old traditions and
modern education
in harmony
in Ladakh*

His father met me and we travelled home in his car. Without seat belts, few signals, over bumpy roads, we avoided pedestrians and animals – it seemed to my somewhat apprehensive view – by a whisker. But we made it – as well as all the succeeding journeys in his car, though I often took a deep breath before climbing in….This was an example of how being in a totally different environment, where accustomed Western rules don't exist, initial alarm can turn into acceptance of a new situation. And that to me was an inner satisfaction and cause of wonder.

I was away from home altogether for two months, and during that time I did not stay even one night in a hotel or guest house, but spent every night in a family's home, paying my way. This I felt was an enormous benefit: not only was I able to absorb and understand more of their culture and way of life, but there was a personal kindness, laughter and fun from the families, which made me feel accepted and liked.

I had come to Ladakh to join a farm project run by the International Society of Ecology and Culture (ISEC is in the reference section). The director, Helena Norberg-Hodge, has made a name for herself in working to resist the pressures of globalisation where large corporations try to elbow out little and local villages, because their end aim is profit, whereas local people in many places all over the world have existed for centuries by building their own houses, producing their own food and existing in a natural, environmentally sound and community based way. Ladakh is a prime example, and whilst the pressure of westernisation has hit them, as it has the rest of the world, ISEC helps them to see the worth of their own culture and traditions, and encourages the making of decisions which take everything into account – including areas where westernization has failed them and this is where they have much to teach us in the West.

The farm project was about participants living in a remote village for one month, with a chosen family, to integrate into their lives and to help on the farm. There were 18 of us volunteers, from Australasia, the Americas and Europe, and each of us went alone into a different family. In my village there were 8 of us, and although we occasionally met up, there was quite a distance of terrain between us, and we had to cope with language difficulties as best we could individually. ISEC had taught us some basic Ladakhi language and some of the younger volunteers mastered this and could carry on some sort of reasonable conversation. Unfortunately, I never did, despite pouring over the phrase sheets, and in the end I had to rely on my gestures, facial expressions, and acting out little scenarios, which caused much hilarity, and occasionally could also be understood….The traditional members of my family did not read or write, but were 'land literate' in a way I was not. Their children had a smattering of English, so this helped from time to time when they visited, and I saved up questions for them. I did discover though, that when non-verbal communication takes place, somehow one often 'met' the person on a different level and even if the wild guessing-game turned out to be wrong, the essential 'meeting' was unimpaired and perhaps deeper as a result.

Back home in the west – perhaps like most of us – I am reasonably clean and tidy most of the time, and I reveled in being muddy and untidy, because washing in the cold stream was quite a performance…. I loved picking weeds and the contact with the earth that gave me, gathering apricots and pitting them, taking the cattle, a cow and dzoma, (a cross between a yak and a cow), to graze, without allowing them to spoil the sharply ripening crops of wheat and barley. I also picked vegetables, learnt how to hand-churn butter, and helped with the meals – all made from scratch three times a day – and these were interspersed with copious cups of sweet milky tea, which they, (mistakenly in my case!), thought westerners preferred to their own salty butter tea. I had made a decision not to ask for any special food whilst I was there, but merely to join in with whatever they ate – mountains of dough, ground in their own mill from the barley they grew into a fine flour called 'tsampa,' the basis for bread and used in vegetable stews, occasionally served with mutton also. Rice and eggs were used but imported from Leh. Rich milk came from the cattle twice a day, and yoghurt and curd cheese supplemented the diet. I also enjoyed the 'chang', the local beer, on occasions. I had a small appetite due to the high altitude, so I only ate a little of everything, including 'paba,' their national dish made of different doughs and very heavy, highly nutritious for Ladakhis.

Whilst living in this village I was lucky to take part in: a showing of Buddhist videos in which the whole village participated; the community funeral of a 70 year old woman villager; and a surprise wedding in my very own family, of the eldest son and his fiancee of two years. These ceremonies helped me to understand more of the culture of the people, and I felt privileged to be included.

Another unexpected happening, from the Muslim family I lived with in Leh, caused me to reflect inwardly, 'Ah! another reason why I am here'… the very first Montessori school in Ladakh, in which my host was the founder and administrator. He invited me to visit the first five little 3 year olds and their young dedicated Montessori trained teacher – and I was impressed and delighted with the school, as the general education for the children in Ladakh is memorizing passages alien to them – or get the stick! I offered to raise funds for the school's expansion when I was back in England. This I am now doing. (See our reference section)

In conclusion I cannot recommend more strongly the benefits of becoming immersed in different cultures and traditions, through meeting with individual people, exchanging with them our differences, and celebrating the common humanity which we share. I returned a stronger and more confident person. The prospect of setting off can be daunting – it was for me – but I trusted my inner conviction and now, some months later, am immeasurably glad that I took the plunge."

Any place may be a pilgrim place and any journey may be a pilgrimage so long as the participant is both focused on the journey and open to surprise.

Stories from some of the Tribal People

We the Yanomami *(population 23,000, Brasil and Venuzuela)*

We are one of the hundreds of different Indian peoples in Amazonia. We hunt fish, gather fruits and keep gardens. we live in large, round, communal homes made of poles and palm-leaf thatch. They open to the sky in the middle and can house up to 400 people. But goldminers enter our land illegally and give us diseases like malaria and flu, which can kill us.

We the Bushmen *(population 95,000 in Angola, Botswana, Namibia, South African Republic, Zambia and Zimbabwe)*

We live in Southern Africa where it's hot and dry and rains only a little. We are many peoples, each speaking a different language, many of which include unusual clicking. we live by hunting animals and gathering wild foods. Our huts are made from branches and thatch. Recently most of our land has been taken by cattle ranchers and we have to work for them, or rely on government hand-outs. In Botswana the government has moved some of us away from our homes in the Kalahari desert, because it wants to mine for diamonds here. But we love this place and we want to stay.

We the Innu *(population 20,000 Canada)*

We are one of the many Indian people in North America. Our land is full of pine forests, fruits and berries, herds of wild caribou and lakes teeming with fish. Until the 1950s we were nomads and followed the caribou herds for meat in the long, cold winters. Now the authorities have made us live in fixed villages. Industries have been set up in our land which has made our lives much harder, and we now suffer from alcoholism and depression. Although Canada is rich, we are poor.

We, the Chukchee *(Population 15,000 Russia)*

We are the tribal peoples in the Siberian tundra. Although this is one of the coldest places on earth, many different tribes live here. We keep reindeer and fish the rivers which are full of salmon. In the 1930s the government began settling us into villages. Now we are poorer, but as long as we can have our lands we will survive.

We, the Jarawa *(population 250-400 India)*

We are nomadic hunter-gathers who live comfortably in forests in the Andaman Islands. When we collect honey we cover our bodies with a plant juice so the bees won't sting us. Until recently we had met few people from outside our tribe. Now settlers from India take our land and carry diseases, like flu, which can kill us.

These stories come from *SURVIVAL* for tribal people. Survival says: Tribal peoples have found ways to live off the land almost everywhere on earth. There are about 300 million tribal people in the world living in thousands of different tribes. As the authors of Travel With Awareness, we ask you our readers to learn more about these people by keeping in touch with Survival. We ask you to travel carefully in areas where tribal people live; shopping with care, consideration and respect for their life-styles.(Contact Survival through our reference section)

Travelling Titbits

Short items of information you may find interesting, useful and fun to read about.

Australia

If you are travelling to Australia look out for Local Exchange Systems production of their own currency, the notes show Australian wildlife and can be recorded as credits or debits.

Bananas

Bananas are one of the most popular fruits, the European union being the largest market. Sadly in most cases the producer of the banana receives only about 5% of the profit. Large amounts of chemicals are used in the production of bananas but is it possible to buy organic ones, they are not necessarily fair-trade. However, large amounts of fair-trade organic bananas are available and some of our supermarkets support and sell these goods.

Beauty

The planet is full of the most beautiful natural objects including the flora and fauna. In recognition of this and as a way of encouraging a new consciousness of the earth the Butterfly Gardeners Association was set up in the USA. Beauty is shown throughout nature and should be celebrated by recognition of its value to peaceful initiatives and by careful preservation of wildlife. More information can be found in the reference section.

Body Shop Awards

Look out for groups nominated by The Body Shop for awards for work with children. In Togo, West Africa, WAO helps child domestic workers. In Tamil Nadu in India, The Peace Trust runs educational programmes for child labourers and provides health care. In Bahia State, Brasil, Movimento de Orgaizacao Communitaria runs programmes to improve education for working children. In Nicaragua Dos Generaciones works for children's rights and provides educational opportunities.

Brasil

The organisation Estrela may be able to offer you a reasonably priced service of local advice, orientation, interpreting, community and cultural visits and family accommodation. Further information about Estrela is in the reference section at the end of the book.

Climate change

It is important to be aware of changes in the climate. Some parts of the world are affected more than others, be prepared. Some problems that may arise: Shortage of snow in the ski resorts; Limited supplies of fresh water; increase in temperatures, a higher heat index putting pressure on supplies of water and on air conditioning; hotter and more penetrating sun which can seriously affect the skin and eyes; it is also possible that there may be more storms and flash floods. Obviously it would be sensible to check out weather forecasts before travelling. Refer to the section on health and fitness in chapter 2 and the kit list at the end of the book.

Compassionate Travellers

In some countries travellers may find animals such as dogs, bears, reptiles, donkeys and so on being unkindly treated. If you do find this please take some action. You may be able to report to the local police or the tourist office. It is best to report locally if possible. If you cannot do this you should take

It is easy and pleasurable to support fair trade.

note of the date and place and perhaps take a photograph and on your return home contact "World Society for the Protection of Animals," WSPA. The contact address is in the reference section at the end of this book. Please avoid having your photograph taken posing with wild animals and avoid hotels that display wild animals. Remember that wild animals are sometimes exploited to bring in tourists.

Fair Trade producers

In some countries it is possible to visit fair-trade producers of some of the goods you buy. Some do not have facilities for visitors but it may be worthwhile trying. Fair-trade goods make excellent presents especially if you can say you saw them being made. See Fair Trade or Traidcraft in the reference section.

Genetically modified crops

Sri Lanka has put a ban on all imports of genetically modified foods. Thailand has stopped the release of all GM crops into the environment.

Globalisation

Around the world the effects of globalisation are becoming more and more obvious and increasingly there is opposition arising and being organised. In countries such as Thailand where the many sweatshop workers are beginning to complain, in India there was a demand for withdrawal from the World Trade organisation, in Brasil landless people occupied a piece of land and in many other countries including, Australia, Kenya, Indonesia you will notice unrest among people in many communities. For the traveller these stirrings may seem insignificant but be aware of them.

Iceland

Iceland has almost no fossil fuel, the country is now trying to run on hydrogen. This could be the world's first hydrogen economy. Check it out in Reykjavik.

India

Look out for organic food in India, but be aware of the growing of GM crops by developers. This is not popular with the local communities.

Ladakh

If you visit Ladakh you may come across Tibetans working on projects concerning the environment. Look out for organic farming, wildlife conservation, energy efficient buildings and training centres run by TEN, Tibetan Environment Network. Contact address in the reference section. Ladakh is coming under severe pressure from tourism, this is having a damaging effect on the way of life of the local people.

Malta, Cyprus and The Greek Islands

If you are visiting these places please look out for trapping of wild birds, the RSPB has had reports from visitors of shooting and trapping of many wild birds. Report to the RSPB, The Lodge, Sandy. Beds. SG19 2DL if you have cause for concern.

Nepal

Many people visit Nepal, if you go the Jampaling you may find a home for elderly Tibetan refugees. They could do with some help and a little goes long way in Nepal.

Norway

If you are in Norway you may hear of the Mayor on a Bench. In Ringerike, mayor Kv Rum may be found sitting on a bench every week meeting people. He has been doing this for six years.

Organic Africa

A number of African countries have received information, advice and resources from the **Henry Doubleday Research Association.** This is intended to empower people, to improve farming systems. In Ghana, the Ghana Organic Agriculture Network has been set up. For further information contact: Overseas Programme, HYDRA, Ryton Organic Gardens, Coventry. CV8 3LG. Tel: 024 7630 3517. E-mail: ove-enquiry@hdra.org.uk   www. Hdra.org.uk

Organic Food

Cuba has developed one of the most efficient organic agriculture systems in the world. The embargos prevented Cuba from importing chemicals and agricultural machinery so the organic route was taken and many small farms have appeared with some 8,000 officially recognised organic gardens in Havana alone.

If you visit China look out for organic food, it has become very popular there.

Poland

Why not spend a holiday on an organic farm in Poland. There are many small eco-farms and you can check this out at Ashoka, Innovators for the public, 1, Curtain Road, London. EC2A 3JX.

It is a sad fact, however, that these wonderful small farms, many using horses to till the land, are under threat from transnational corporations, globalisation and the proposed enlargement of the European Union. The International Coalition to protect the Polish countryside has been set up and if you wish for more information contact ECEAT- Poland, 34-146 Stryszow 156, Poland. Tel/fax +48 33 879 7114

Power generation

Look out for small wind turbines fitted to roofs of houses or other buildings, this is a very economical way to generate power for family use, They can be seen in Spain. In Germany look for solar systems on roofs, also in Israel new buildings must install solar systems for supplying hot water.

Railways

Most travellers pass through railway stations at some stage of their journey. Look out for children who are living in and around railway stations. You sometimes see them in bus stations also. In India, Bangladesh, Kenya, Mexico, Peru and the UK, you may come across The Railway Children, a charity working to help these children. You can find information about this organisation in the reference section at the end of the book.

Rainbows

Rainbows have been seen as a way of connecting the young with the old, the near with the far, the familiar and the strange, the known and the unknown. The Rainbow project, beginning in Switzerland has extended to other countries. For information on the project contact: Rainbow Project, CH-3433 Schwenden, Switzerland. Tel: +44 34 461 31 01. E-mail: rainbowproject@bluewin.ch www.Rainbowproject.ch

Rainforest

Uncontrolled logging in precious rainforests can devastate areas that we cannot afford to lose. In Canada an agreement has been signed by timber merchants, environmentalists and indigenous Indians to preserve some 2.5 million acres on the Pacific coast. The agreement covers British Columbia's Central and North coast rainforests known as the Great Bear Rainforests. One of the rare species of bears found there is the Kermode or Spirit Bear.

"Reality Tours"

In America it is possible to sign up for a holiday with a difference. Groups of people are choosing to visit some of the most politically delicate parts of the world. The tours are planned with the idea of allowing people to encounter some of the problems experienced by the local population. The tours can be very hard-going as the tourists may have live under basic conditions, perhaps sleeping on floors and certainly sampling the local foods. It is difficult to say how spontaneous the encounters are, the trips have to be well organised beforehand.

Russia

The wonderful Kitezh Ecovillage Community for children in Russia is a project assisting children many of whom have been rescued from orphanages. With help from a Scottish charity it has almost doubled in size and now provides support to an increasing number of children. For information write to Ecological Trust, 66, The Park, Forres, Moray. Scotland 1V36 3TZ. Tel 01309 690995.

The Salvation Army

Not many people realise that The Salvation Army reaches out into many parts of the world. Keep a look out, you may come across them on your travels.

Shopping abroad

It is always good to bring back some presents purchased while abroad but please shop with awareness. Look at the labels, think about the price, especially if it is very cheap. In some parts of the world there is a great deal of exploitation. In the Indian sub-continent children as young as six may be used to help make carpets, in many instances the maker of the goods earns next to nothing and the middle-person takes the bulk of the profit. Be aware that many forms of slavery exist in most parts of the world. If you can buy direct from the producer or if you seek advice before you visit a country, then you may be able to support the local people and help stamp out slave labour and exploitation. Contact Anti-Slavery International for advice, or Traidcraft. Read New Internationalist August 2001. Information about these can be found in the reference section at the end of this book. See also chapter 5 Home Again.

Social Inventions

There is an award scheme for social inventions and there is also a **Global Ideas Bank**. Full information on this can be found from: The Institute of Social Inventions, 20, Heber Road, London. NW2 6AA. Tel: 0208 208 2853. E-mail: rhino@dial.pipex.com

Sri Lanka

Cities of Anuradhapura and Polonnaruwa have sites of very important historical interest, parts dating back to the 4th century B.C. and the height of Buddhist civilisation. However a look behind the scenes will tell another story today. Farmers are suffering badly, they are not getting a fair price for their crops and are unable to cover their costs, many of them have committed suicide. Do please take a little time to talk with local farmers and offer support to them.

Tanzania

Waitrose is selling organic cotton wool, it is supplied by smallholding farmers in Tanzania, part of the price is used to support the farmers.

Time

"The European and the African have an entirely different concept of time. In the European worldview, time exists outside man, exists objectively, and has measurable and linear characteristics. According to Newton, time is absolute: "Absolute, true, mathematical time of itself and from its own nature, it flows equably and without relation to anything external." The European feels himself to be time's slave, dependent on it, subject to it. To exist and function, he must observe its iron clad, inviolate laws, its inflexible principles and rules. He must heed deadlines, dates, days and hours. He moves within the rigours of time and cannot exist outside them. They impose upon him their requirements and quotas. An unresolvable conflict exists between man and time, one that always ends with man's defeat – time annihilates him.

Africans apprehend time differently. For them, it is a much looser concept, more open, elastic, subjective. It is man who influences time, its shape, course and rhythm, (man acting, of course, with the consent of gods and ancestors). Time is even something that man can create outright, for time is made manifest through events, and whether an event takes place or not depends, after all, on man alone. If two armies do not engage in a battle, then that battle will not occur (in other words, time will not have revealed its presence, will not have come into being).

Time appears as a result of our actions, and vanishes when we neglect or ignore it. It is something that springs to life under our influence, but falls into a state of hibernation, even non-existence, if we do not direct our energy towards it. It is a subservient, passive essence, and, most importantly, one dependent on man. The absolute opposite of time as it is understood in the European worldview. In practical terms, this means that if you go to a village where a meeting is scheduled for the afternoon but find no one at the appointed spot, asking, "When will the meeting take place?" makes no sense. You know the answer: "It will take place when people come."

This item is included by kind permission of Allen Lane, the Penguin Press and Liepman AG. It is taken from "The Shadow of the Sun. My African Life," by Ryszard Kapuscinski.

Transport

Transport is the fastest growing area of oil use. Around the world there are some 500 to 600 million cars. The use of cars consumes around 60% of global oil production. In addition, cars put into the atmosphere huge amounts of pollution. When you travel at home or in a foreign country why not try the local transport, it can be more fun than your own or hire car, and much more environmentally friendly. Even better, try walking or cycling if possible, you may be able to hire cycles or even buy them (sell before returning home), in this way you will see more and keep healthy on local trips around your base. Note; in France, near Nice, there is the first purpose-built factory for the manufacture of air-powered cars. Keep a look out for them.

Turkey

Check up on Turkey's nutty products. The largest producer of hazelnuts, Turkey could produce large amounts of hydrogen by incinerating hazelnuts. This could drive the new hydrogen fuelled BMWs.

Photographs: Ailsa Moore, Barbara Butler

Clean Water

Water

Climate change and increasing demands on supplies of water are putting extra strain on adequate provision to local populations in many parts of the world. In some popular tourist areas the visitors use so much water in swimming pools and showers that the local population is deprived of adequate supplies. Please be aware of this and where possible moderate your use of water and possibly even make a donation to Water Aid. (address in the reference section at the end of the book.)

Note: 40% of the world's population has no access to clean drinking water, for example in Kenya only about 44% are supplied, in China it is about 67% and in Brasil 76%. We take supplies of water for granted but for many people water is a very precious commodity.

In Sweden the annual 'pee outside day' in Sigmota , saves 50% of the water usually used in toilet flushing.

In India there is a widespread shortage of water. India has over 4,000 large dams. The Narmada river in central India has many dams and the development of even more, threatens the homes and livelihoods of millions of people. Read New Internationalist July 2001 edition to find out more.

Some of the information contained in these titbits has come from the publication
LIVING LIGHTLY with POSITIVE NEWS. This excellent magazine comes out four times a year and can be contacted at no. 5 Enterprise Centre, Clun, Shropshire, SY7 8NF.
Telephone: 0845 458 4758. Fax: 0845 458 4759
Email: office@positivenews.org.uk   www.positivenews.org.uk

Travellers' Tales

Chapter Four

Travellers Tales

'All genuine knowledge originates in direct experience.'
Mao Tse-tung.

Hospitality in Krajina

Ailsa Moore

On a visit to Krajina in Croatia during the conflict in Bosnia, I visited a group of displaced Serb people. These lovely, elderly people had lost their homes because of shelling in the place where they lived. They were now housed in a container unit. The container units were tin huts which were scorchingly hot at times, having almost no ventilation. I arrived at the door to find a jumper sleeve laid down outside. It was the custom to have a small mat outside the front door to clean shoes before entering the room. I used the sleeve and a dear, wrinkled face greeted me, the lady of the house beckoned me in, her husband stood by. We had no common language, but clasped hands and passed on a message of greeting. There was nothing in the container unit except a bed, no food or drink, so what could my hosts do. The lady of the house drew me in and with a careful hand smoothed a place on the bed for me to sit. That graceful act of hospitality was so typical and if this couple had had food they would have offered it, even if it was their last crumb. It is hard to find the equivalent of this experience in the wealthy, materialistic parts of the world, but it gives a richness to encounters sadly often unknown in the affluent world.

Egyptian Monasteries

Roger Millman

The village of El Saraqna is close to the monastery where we stayed, El Muharraq. The journey to the village took us two hours in a mini-bus... we walked to the house where the Coptic Evangelical Social Services, (CEOSS), had their headquarters. We spent some time in prayer in English and in Arabic with the local workers. We were then taken onto the roof where we could appreciate the good views of the narrow streets and alleyways nearby. We then went for a walking tour of the village, during which Samuel, from Kenya, and I had a ride on a donkey and raised a laugh amongst the watching villagers..We were shown a village woman's home, where CEOSS had installed a toilet hole connecting up with a proper sewer. I felt uncomfortable as we seemed to invade her house.

"on our last full day in Egypt we were collected by Miriam and Nabil and we set off along the desert road towards Alexandria. We turned off the main road and crossed the desert. We were given an extensive tour of Barramos Monastery... some of the monks live as hermits in caves nearby. It was almost impossible for us to walk to the cave because the wind had developed into a sandstorm.. Altogether we visited four monasteries.

A Kenyan in Britain

I came from Kenya to a Christians Aware International Gathering in Britain... We arrived at Rydal from Skipton... Rydal is one of the most beautiful places in the Lake District, and Rydal Hall, where we stayed, is surrounded by beautiful mountains and trees. A river flows near to where we stayed.

We visited Stool Farm in Great Langdale…despite the cold the sheep were grazing and surprising for us from Kenya were the dogs whose duty is to chase the sheep from one field to another and up the hills…we enjoyed and appreciated the warm welcome and concern.'

Waiting

Ailsa Moore

I was on my way to India, travelling alone as usual, I had already sent the relevant information to my Tibetan friends to say when I would be arriving at Delhi airport, of course it was in the early hours! I arrived on time, my hope was to travel with my friends to Rajpur in North East India. I searched among the hordes of locals meeting people off the flight, no sign of my friends, never mind they may have been held up. I saw a waiting room on the other side of the now almost deserted road, I paid to go in and found a seat, but would my friends know I was in there? I then found that if you came out you had to pay to enter again! This I sorted out with the kindly man on the door. I waited on, I did have a packet of biscuits in my bag, there was no food available. One biscuit an hour I thought, the bottle of water gave me several sips an hour. I waited. A kind man sitting next to me asked about my situation, I explained, he thought I should find hotel, but I knew this would not work, how would my friends find me. The man offered to buy me a coffee from a small stand in the corner, very welcome. I tied my bags to my leg and dozed off. To visit the loo you had to go out of the waiting room, another smile from the doorman, then I found my large bag wouldn't go through the loo door, the coffee man looked after it, I then looked after his bags for the same reason.

Hours were passing, my friends must have got the time wrong. Dawn broke, by now I had a list of my options. My coffee friend had gone to his plane, the doorman became worried, I felt relaxed I promised him my friends would come. After some ten hours, I thought it possible that my friends had mixed up the clock times, perhaps they were twelve hours out. I must go out when twelve hours had passed and look, it was now mid-day. No sign, the milling throng showed no sign of a Tibetan dress, then I saw one. At last, but no it wasn't my friend. Should I go up to her and ask for help, she was obviously meeting somebody else. Quickly before she left, I was certain she would speak English and I knew she was from Tibet because of her apron, a beautiful hand-made apron worn by married Tibetan women. I asked if she had seen a Tibetan lady in the airport, she said no, but she would look, she went all over the waiting area but to no avail. Who was I waiting for? I told her, I know that lady she said, my heart lifted. Well she said, as I know her I will look after you, and that she did. I was taken to her home, given lunch and while I was eating it she went to her office to 'phone all round Delhi to see if she could locate my friends, you must stay here if I can't find them she had said. I felt really wanted. Eventually my friends were found and I was taken to meet them. They had been given the wrong arrival day by the advice centre, there was great rejoicing and I was treated like a queen. Hospitality of a special kind.

An Encounter of a Special Kind in Afghanistan

This is an extract from the book "An Unexpected Light" by Jason Elliot and is included here by kind permission of the publishers, Picador. The details of this book are to be found in the reference section at the end of our book.

I was about to leave when an icy gust of wind swept into the room. Four men appeared at the door. They sat down cross-legged a few feet away on the opposite platform, the fresh snow clinging to their eyebrows and beards. Two of them carried automatic rifles. The third unslung a light machine gun, rested the barrel on its bipod, and eased from his neck a twenty foot long ammunition belt which slithered in coils like an anaconda down onto the carpet. The fourth carried nothing, wore a plain white turban and dark *pattu,* and sat down a few feet from me with an air of both dignity and calm.

He was obviously their commander, and his appearance was so striking I caught myself staring. His brow was broad and unlined and his narrow face tapered downwards from high cheekbones towards a rich black beard. A pair of dark oval eyes, as kindly as they were intense, strengthened the dove like impression of his features.

His face was not only beautiful but seemed to emanate an extraordinary purity, an interior integrity with which I associated profound goodness. It did not seem properly to belong to my own world, which was perhaps its fascination, and the sight of it was like a gem flashing from layers of worthless stone. And I was staring not just because his face was utterly unlike the faces I knew from home, but because I felt all of a sudden that if I were to attach myself to him, apprentice-like, and follow him to his home and enter into his life and language and hardships and battles and pleasures, I might learn something substantial about the country and its culture and all that was hidden from the casual onlooker I really felt myself to be, able only to observe what was most superficial. And I felt too with equal certainly, based on nothing but that glance, that had I made the suggestion he would have agreed and honoured the spirit of the impulse without question.

He acknowledged me with the faintest of smiles and an almost imperceptible nod, and our worlds were momentarily bridged. A glimmer of questioning in his eyes told me he was as intrigued about the solitary foreigner as was I about him. And thus passed our moment of exchange, which was not shared by his men, who eyed me with the usual reserve and curiosity. Yet I knew I couldn't stay.

I record this only because it was, in a sense, an incident I was beginning to recognize as typical of the place, as characteristic of encounters with individuals as with the landscape itself. Always there was this flash of beauty out of the backdrop of harshness, like a ray of light thrown across a cave; a drop of sweetness distilled from the sea of indifferent experience, prompting feelings which, if translated into physical terms, were the equivalent of glimpsing a fertile and delicately cultivated valley after hours of walking through barren mountains; feelings of tremendous relief and affirmation which carried with them the scent of a different way of living, to which the usual contraints of life would not really apply. In time, such moments were insubstantial, but in memory proved ineradicable; they awoke different urges which if laid bare would appear as madness to the ordinary world. And this was a large part of the magic of the place and its people; one might follow such promptings and not be considered mad. To be true to such moments, recklessly true perhaps, was the challenge, the parting of the ways, that travel throws into one's path; and I was deeply disappointed with myself for having let it pass.

Doctor in Uganda

To mark the United Nations International Year of the family. **Dr. Barbara Tonge** *made a three month visit to Uganda as part of the Christians Aware programme. A British GP, she threw herself into a demanding programme of health education and simple health care in rural Uganda, making a gift of her skills and expertise.*

"What is immediately obvious," she commented in a recent article, is the central importance of family life in African culture. But it is under threat: under threat from messages brought in by mass communications and the dominance of market forces, and under threat as a consequence of the AIDS epidemic. After decades of civil war Uganda is experiencing a recovery, but is still quite unable to deliver basic health care at affordable rates for all her people. This, with the eroding effect of HIV infection in Uganda today, is putting families and indeed whole communities at risk.

She writes:

> Good family life is a cause for celebration: it is seen in its fullness in Ugandan society. Love of children, a place for children in the family and the community, are both traditional, as is a sense of belonging through contributing, a known pattern of upbringing and behaviour. All children need the sense of identity and self respect given by a positive role in society, and a conviction they are wanted and needed. We in the so-called developed World would do well to look at this pattern of behaviour when so many of our young people are unemployed, marginalized and unwanted, lacking a sense of identity and a role in society.

In Uganda, as the **AIDS** epidemic decimates a whole generation, the number of orphans has soared. In one district of Uganda alone-Rakai there are an estimated 58,000 orphans. There is a threat that many children may be isolated in orphanages, or may become second class citizens in their families of adoption. This in some ways reflects a global issue. Vast numbers of children are being born into a world that does not "need"them, but exploits them.

In social terms, the burden of orphans and the loss of young adults with skills and training is all important. Grandparents find themselves responsible for as many as ten grandchildren, perhaps twenty years after rearing their own children.

The physical labour and the sorrow that go with this situation can hardly be imagined.

Visit to Peru

Rosemary Kelham

I have wanted to meet the Incas ever since I was in the Infant school. I was already reading fluently when I started school at the age of four and was fortunate to have a teacher, Miss Fazey, who brought me material from her own library to maintain my love of books and extend the range of my reading. That was my first meeting with the Incas, although for a while they were confused with Hiawatha who occurred in the same volume and was coloured in with the same set of crayons.

The second meeting happened last year when, at long last, I took the journey to Peru.

I thought I knew all about these people by then but no amount of reading prepares you for your encounter with these lovely kind, patient and gentle people with their quiet humour and sense of fun. Their life, whether as plainsmen or High Andeans is hard and moments of relaxation are scarce. The two different physical environments have produced two different physical types. The plainsmen are taller and leaner with a uniform complexion. Although only eleven degrees from the equator the coastal strip is never unbearably hot as the cold Humboldt current sweeps up the coast and keeps Lima under constant cloud. They expect about an hour of sunshine each day. It does not rain either - or rarely. Rain comes once every hundred years and the last shower was only eighty years ago. Everything depends on irrigation and the rain that falls in the High Andes. A dry Winter means traffic jams as everyone rushes home from work to use the water that is turned on for two hours in the evening. The High Andeans are short and barrel-chested with bright rosy cheeks. This is due to the thin atmosphere and they have developed huge lungs and overlarge hearts to cope with the shortage of oxygen. They also have 20% more red blood cells than normal. Their work is physically very hard and life expectancy about 57 years. They feel dizzy at lower levels just as we and the Limans feel the effects of altitude.

The Spaniards appliqued Western civilisation and religion onto the Inca culture and the stitches still show. A large part of the Catholic church built over the Temple of the Moon in Cusco fell down at the last earthquake and it is possible to see the two together. The stark simplicity of the temple with its empty trapezoidal niches contrasts sharply with the ornate and showy decoration in the church. One wall of the temple would have had a huge gold sunburst on it, but this was melted down by the Spaniards and the Incas forbidden to worship the sun any more. The niches had once contained the mummified remains of the Inca "saints" and these had been paraded before the folk every year. The Spaniards decreed that Christian saints should be paraded instead an the Inca mummies disappeared from view but not from practice. The cross on the high altar boasts the Inca sun behind it and the effigies of the Madonna all have triangular skirts. I am told, by Juan, that the Incas slipped the mummies under the triangular skirt so that they were still paraded because to see such a parade was to be blessed for the year. "Of course," he said, " it is so much easier now." "Because Christianity is well-established?" I asked. "Not that!" he said shocked, "You don't hve to turn out now. You get blessed just the same if you see it on television."

The Uros Indians on their floating islands on Lake Titicaca high in the Andes have the same happy knack of mixing Ancient and Modern. Their islands are built up of tortora reed which is cut from the lake and lashed together to form platforms three feet thick. Houses and the one school are also made of the reed. They have to add another layer to it every three months or so. When you step ashore the whole island rocks and walking from one side to the other is a strange experience. The ladies spread their goods on blankets and sit behind them on the "ground". On my visit they were enjoying huge ice-creams and one of the party asked where they had them from. A lady pointed to the reed hut behind her. "Can we buy them there?" she was asked. She shook her head and took another mighty lick. "Freezer very small." she said. How do you get a freezer on a floating island? It seems that an enterprising German salesman went out to the islands and persuaded the inhabitants of this one to invest in solar panels. Small deposit and seven years to pay. They will own their panels in 2005. I looked into one tiny hut and there was a Baby Belling boiling ring and a 26" television set with just enough room to sit in front of it. The Lake is some sixty miles long and the bottom end, about fifteen miles of it, is in Bolivia. The local politics are volatile to say the least. The islands are now tethered to stakes driven into the bed of the lake since a storm in the winter of 1999 caused one set of islanders to wake up in Bolivia. Hilda, my informant , smiled a slow gentle smile as she said: "Took them a month to sail it back. For the last bit someone lent them an outboard motor."

Inland from Lake Titicaca, the highest navigable lake in the world, and climbing yet higher lie the peasant farms of the Alto Plano. The mountainsides rising above the High Plain are a chequerboard of cultivated strips running in different directions. I suddenly realised that I was looking at the Peruvian version of the medieval Three Field System. The depth of soil, where it exists at all, varies greatly and each farmer has little strips of good bad and indifferent. The farmer who welcomed folk into his home was living the same life as his Inca ancestors. His daughter was about to marry and the adobes, cut from the local claybed, were stacked in the yard to dry and ready to build a new room for the couple. Like the Incas of old the present day folk still build each room as a separate unit and to get from one room to another always have to go outside. There is no such thing as a connecting door. Even in the city of Cusco this is often the case. On this farm bedroom and living room were one. The farmer sat on his bed, beaming at these wonderful guests who had honoured him with a visit. The guests were actually feeling a little self-conscious and intrusive. He proudly showed us the certificates gained by his son and pinned above his bed. This was a large sack stuffed with straw and reeds and placed directly on the earthen floor. Handwoven blankets and llama skins were piled on top and he showed us how he went to bed in winter wearing his boots and woolly hat and rolled himself in the skins for warmth. In pride of place on the wall, even outshining the certificates, was his wife's new hat. The farm had shown a small profit for the year and he had spent it on a new bowler for his wife. "Very hard! Rain and things fall on her and she not hurt." He showed us how he tilled the unforgiving soil. A broad spade would be useless here. He had a long piece of wood, about six inches wide, and on one end was fastened a narrow piece of a harder wood. This was shaped to a taper but not a point. It had the effect of a pickaxe but was used like a spade. This was the tool he used to dig his fields up and down the mountains, leaving the house in the dark so as to start work as soon as it was light and returning when it was too dark to work. He had some llamas and two bulls and these were in the care of his wife. She sat out on the plain all day watching the stock and doing her knitting or crochet. The weekly market was the high point of her existence when she met another woman and had someone to share a conversation. The new room , when built, would have a topping out ceremony when a cross would be placed on the apex as a blessing. To be quite sure of the blessing there would be models of the two bulls as well! An Inca doesn't take risks.

My meeting with the Incas far outshone everything that I had dared to hope for it and I was left in no doubt that all Incas are Peruvians but not all Peruvians are Incas.

India – Fragments of Hope
Barbara Butler

One statue in the grounds of Santiniketan stands out for me, from the many fine sculptures on the perhaps unique campus of the university founded by Rabindranath Tagore in 1921 as a place of excellence in the arts for people from all over the world. It is the statue of a student by Ram Kinkar Beij but it has, very unusually, had a bowl of rice pudding placed on the head of the student by Nanda Lal Bose, so that it has become Sujata, who took rice to Buddha whilst he was meditating.

A student with a bowl of rice pudding to give in service of another conveys a whole, wholesome and even holy message, a message which people visiting India from the West have come to almost expect to find during their travels. The man perhaps most responsible for this expectation was Vivekenanda, who might be called the first Hindu missionary to the West. He attended and spoke at the World parliament of Religions in 1893 and who set up the Ramakrishna Mission and the Vedanta societies in Europe and America. Vivekananda appealed for people to live whole, wholesome and holy lives by linking their meditation and study to disinterested service for and with people in the world. His appeal, for contemplation and action, for work and worship, or work as worship, has been taken up by other world famous Indian religious leaders and philosophers including Rabinranath Tagore and Mahatma Gandhi. Gandhi was convinced that religion could not be separated from life and that the religious person, of any faith tradition, must attend to the needs of his or her neighbour and that if this was done then human barriers would be broken down and human development and equality would occur naturally.

Visitors to India in the 1990s myself included, may be sadly disappointed to find a country which seems at first glance to lack anything of the wholeness, wholesomeness and holiness envisaged by its famous sages, a land where people are divided, sometimes violently, the rich from the poor, caste from caste, and people of faith from each other, into their own inward-looking communities. The shadow of Aodhya both bolsters up those who fuel the furnaces of communalism and smothers those who work for reconciliation and peace.

I have made two recent visits to India, the first, in August 1993, to Bangalore, following in the footsteps of Vivekananda, to attend the "Sarva Dharma Sammelana" on the hundredth anniversary of the first Parliament of Religions. The second visit, in January 1994, was a Christians Aware group venture to link communities and friends in Orissa and Calcutta. It was during my second visit, whilst the group was travelling by train from Calcutta to Tagore's Santiniketan, " abode of peace", that a quarrel followed by a serious fight broke out between some of the passengers. The jolting of the train was matched by the jolting of the group's expectations in making the journey, especially when told that we very lucky to emerge unscathed from the incident.

The presence of the poor in India, so many and so suffering, provides a constantly jarring note for visitors and Indians alike. Roughly the top 10percent of the population is rich by any standards, whilst 47 percent of the people live below the subsistence level. Ill health is normal for the poor people. I spent half a day in a mobile medical clinic, travelling to the area South of Calcutta, where I saw many varieties of painful skin rashes and drooping jaundice victims at very close quarters. Polio and leprosy are common and cancer cases are increasing in urban areas. The age of death is around fifty years for the majority of India's poor people and the infant death rate is high.

The CA group visited Mother Theresa's home for dying destitutes, where an average of six people die every day, and where six more replace them from the streets of Calcutta. Food and clothing are scarce in the poor communities. In our recent visit to Orissa we met tribal people who have either one garment per person or no clothes at all. Tribals, about forty five million people, are normally marginalized in India, which is why the work of the Society for Developmental Action and others like it is vital for the future. The debts of village people have increased, in many cases forcing them into the towns to add to the problem of slums, shanties and unemployment. The starkest picture of the division between rich and poor India was painted for me when I visited a new Dam in Orissa with the CA group. The Dam is being financed by the World Bank, and will provide hydro-electricity and irrigation for a large area. The construction is beautiful at first glance but a closer second glance reveals the way in which it is being erected, by the day in and day out drudgery of the poor people of the area, men, women and even children. Recently, we were told, six hundred people were killed in a tunnel.

Signs of wholeness, wholesomeness and holiness are not very clear in modern India and sometimes they are so hidden that the traveller may miss them altogether, cocooned inside one of the many and varied religious havens, or alternatively whilst wandering around in a smog of noise and quarrel. Such experiences of India, floating well above the reality of the country and its people, which we were at times in danger of doing at the Bangalore gathering, or walking the very real and very grim and polluted streets of Calcutta, observing the paintless and dilapidated buildings and the emaciated majority of the people, some pulling rickshaws, some begging and many just existing, are disjointed and often depressing.

But the most un-promising exteriors to western eyes, ears and noses may hide interiors of great interest and great beauty. The most dusty and noisy Calcutta Street may lead, often through a grubby doorway and a dark dank stairway, to a hive of faith-filled, loving and dedicated activity with and on behalf of the people of India. It is possible to have a glimpse of wholeness, wholesomeness and holiness in such places, and to realise that there is hope for the future.

An un-promising Calcutta doorway leads up a narrow stairway to the "silence community of those" ..who neither hear nor speak except visually and others who cannot go places except in their imaginations and yet who aspire towards self-sufficiency." The community now numbers 72 people who work together and earn their livings producing greetings cards, incense sticks, candles, jewellery and wooden decorations. There is also an impressive computer service. The Indian council of rehabilitation and Sports for the disabled exhibits a shabby exterior, but once inside the building the visitor is taken aback by the atmosphere of love and service, cultivated over 16 years of painstaking and dedicated work by Tapan Dhar and his co-workers. Over 17,000 disabled people from all over India are enrolled with the council – Seminars and conferences are organised, advice is given, skills are taught and handicrafts are being developed. The council offers opportunities in sporting activities, and sent a team to the Paralympics in 1988.

One of the most inspiring sights to be seen on a visit to Calcutta is that of the slum children studying in the Young Men's Welfare Society night schools. 1,200 children attend these schools and study as they would in a normal primary school, except that they go to school during the night, when they are free from daytime labours. The classrooms, some in fee-paying school buildings, are bright, and the children and parents are highly motivated. YMWS has raised some scholarships for the academic children to go on to secondary and even higher education. The teachers are involved in the communities as well as in the schools, and they receive regular training. The CA group visited a "pavement school" in a bustee which offered pre-primary education to children crowded together on the dusty and narrow floor, polluted by passing traffic and with little equipment, but with all the children listening intently to the teacher.

Many people of all faiths in India are working with children and young people for education, training and a future in recognition of... " everyone's basic freedom and rights, in recognition of the world's humanity." The Ramakrishna Mission, where the CA group stayed in Calcutta, is well known for its

112

YMWS school children at St. Lawrence School, Calcutta

113

work in education and the development of young people, and offers a wide range of educational opportunities up to post graduate levels and including specialist institutions in science and agriculture. During the "Sarva Dharma Sammelana" a large group visited the Maha Bodi Society in Bangalore and met the children from poor families who are educated in the society's school. A group also visited two Christian projects for the more than forty thousand children who live in Bangalore, where they are being offered accommodation, education, training and loving support.

The YMWS is one of Christians Aware's oldest overseas link organisations. It is a society of Hindus, Muslims and Christians, all working together in Calcutta and the surrounding countryside with the aim of empowering the people with the skills and abilities to develop in their own way. The influence of Canon Subir Biswas of Calcutta Cathedral, who opened the Cathedral to the Coty in the 1970's, was great in the development of YMWS. It was a delight to learn that YMWS now gives priority to girl's education, because studies have shown that if girls are educated the whole level of society is likely to be raised, for... "a country can't progress by neglecting its womenfolk, just as a bird can't fly without one of its wings". A special effort is being made by YMWS to offer education to Muslim girls. A secondary night school has been started for older Muslim girls who are not expected to attend "mixed" schools. The school demands high standards and the girls are keen to reach them. A Muslim girl led the YMWS section of the Independence Day parade this year.

The first undertaking of the Society of Developmental Action in Orissa was the building and development of a girls secondary school in Kuliana, a school for tribal children who would otherwise have had no education at all. The school is flourishing and SODA has gone on to develop programmes for tribal women's development, including legal training and health education, a family counselling programme and an orphanage. The orphanage of sixty eight children, is a simple place of love and hope. Currently SODA is working with tribal people in remote areas in the south of Orissa in raising awareness of the reality of poverty and marginalisation and in articulating hopes for the future.

The CA group attended a large gathering of some four hundred people of the Didai tribe who had recently shared an awareness raising programme, who know very well what is needed for their future and who are prepared to work for it with SODA. It was the women of the tribe, of whom four percent are literate, who came forward to explain that their children frequently cannot attend the only school because because they have no clothes to wear. They must walk a long way to reach a clinic and that they often eat only leaves.

The contrast between the Didai people, who are preparing to pick up the burden of the responsibility for their own future, and another tribe we visited, could not have been starker. The second tribe has not shared an awareness raising course, and appeared sad, with sickly children and violent and drunken men and women. Contact and working together with others for the future are clearly needed in the second tribe and in many others.

In my two recent visits to India, in the midst of the dominating climate of division, struggle and suffering, I have encountered many faith-filled, loving dedicated people and communities for whom there is no dichotomy between the sacred and the secular, who are somehow managing to combine work and worship, and who offer a glimpse, however fleeting and however dim, into the possibility of the whole, wholesome and holy India, where not only students but a whole cross section of people, of all castes and classes and tribes, are enabled to carry a bowl of rice pudding to another, to make their contribution to their community, country and world.

One of Rabindranath Tagore's poems tells of a poor beggar woman in the streets of Calcutta who asks a passing prince to give her something. He asks her, "what have you to give to me?" She tells him that she has nothing, but he insists, and she gives him a small grain of rice. That evening she

People at Work in Pakistan

takes out the wooden bowl of rice, her only food, to prepare her meagre supper. In the middle of the rice she discovers a mine of pure gold, of exactly the size of the grain of rice she gave to the prince. She weeps, as she realises that she, poor as she is, could have given more, could have done more, and that she would thereby have been enriched.

Visit to Pakistan
Jeanne Coker

The Christians Aware visit which Jeanne joined was arranged with the Ockenden Venture in the UK and Pakistan. Hospitality was given by members of the diocese of Peshawar with the help of Mano Ramashah, the bishop at the time. Andrew Ashdown led the group.

Whenever I travel to a new country I always have a some preconceived ideas, usually planted in my mind by a few unrelated facts and half remembered stories told by other travellers. So what did I expect in Pakistan? Hot and poor; dominated by Islam and full of political upheaval; a young country with lots of Afghan refugees.

Yes, it was hot! and areas of Pakistan are very poor but in Lahore where we spent a day sight-seeing and in Peshawar where we stayed for two weeks there was much more prosperity than I expected. The bazaars were full of all sorts of goods and I could quite happily have spent many days wandering around them. I did buy some beautiful cotton material and had it made up by the local tailor all for £10. On the train journey from Lahore to Rawalpindi we saw many miles of fertile plains (and the largest rice field I have ever seen). On one of our visits out of Peshawar we were driven through the fertile area to the North of the city. But the purpose of our visit was to see the refugee camps and find out what was happening there. We found a barren wasteland where every drop of water had to be brought in by tanker. Each camp was different but the refugees, with help from a variety of sources, were working hard to make permanent homes and to develop a sustainable lifestyle. However, let me start at the beginning.

Conflict in Afghanistan started in the late 70's and by 1984 there were about 3.5 million refugees in and around Peshawar. This compares with a local population of about 2.25 million. About 1.9 million remain with maybe half a million unregistered (this means no food card). There was renewed fighting in 1992 so there were "new" refugees. The first camp we visited was permanent with a population of about 30,000. They had built their own homes and ran their own shops and were responsible for law and order. They had been in this camp for ten years or more. We visited the school there which was very basic. The only display material was a cartoon style drawn warning of the dangers of mines. The teachers come from another camp and had been there about six years, some are highly qualified.

At the next camp we went to see the women's sewing and knitting classes. Slipper socks now have a whole new meaning! We saw the beginners class and the next stage of progression. Attendance at classes was meticulously recorded. Men were building houses and there was a "seedling" programme to provide bushes and trees in this barren place.

Our last visits to camps were about 50km out of the city and were the original camps. I found this very depressing. Here was a stark landscape with tumble down houses built by the first refugees who have since returned to Afghanistan. There were clusters of repaired houses where the newcomers were living and here and there brave displays of greenery. We went with two of the women organisers to collect finished craftwork for sale in the shops. No false sentimentality there; only perfect goods were accepted and there seemed to be great deal of bargaining going on about the price. We played with children while this was going on; they were lively and alert and seemed very healthy. At the second camp war-orphaned boys, aged 12 upwards, made carpets under adult supervision. By this age there is little opportunity for any schooling and they need to have a way of sustaining themselves in the future when hopefully they will return "home".

We visited the Sandy Gall hospital where everybody was busy making artificial limbs and wheel chairs, getting people mobile again. This was a place of great hope. For most people the worst is over, the physical wounds have healed, most of the pain has gone and they can live mainly independent lives. There was a training programme for physiotherapists (for whom there is an ENORMOUS need), from four areas of Afghanistan. The trainees travelled to Peshawar across the border without passports and through fighting. In the physiotherapy department I also saw one of the saddest people, a woman who had recently arrived with a bullet in her head and part of her skull missing. There was brain damage causing some paralysis to her left side. Three of her children had been killed. She had her five other children with her but had no home and they mainly slept in mosques. Will she and her family have a future?

There were visits to the dental hospital and then to the children's hospital which had no patients because the money had run out. We heard about the move to reduce aid to persuade Afghans to return to their own country but the fighting continued and many, many of the anti-personnel mines remain. Some were designed to attract children!

And what of the people? We met many highly qualified people unable to make use of their qualifications: teachers at the basic school, a doctor acting as a dental nurse, a French graduate shaping material for artificial limbs. "Limb disabled" are calculated to be 1 in 12 of the population. I was amazed at the organisation that provided food and water for all these people and the enormous amount of work done by caring people throughout the world. And not least, the people of Pakistan. No restrictions had been put on the refugees in the country. They could travel freely, find work if they could, often buy or rent houses. It was thought that some ten percent had integrated into the local community in Peshawar. What generosity in a poor country!

And in the midst of learning about and sharing with refugees we took a day off and went up the Khyber Pass; a real feat of engineering with the railway criss-crossing in and out of the mountains, tall bridges over deep valleys. It is knee deep in history from Alexander the Great to the British colonists then to Pakistan and now to the sad people of Afghanistan. We went close to the border and looked across the valley to two serene villages, one in Pakistan and the other Afghanistan.

Muslim Girls in School

Christians Aware Visit to Lebanon – 1997
Joan Dorrell

Beirut is an ancient and noble city dating back to prehistory. Today, it is battle-scarred, and swarming with cars. The city environs rise like the sides of a bowl up the surrounding hills. From 2500 feet above the harbour there are unique views of an aquamarine sea and fir clad heights. At night, the lights of villages twinkle around this immense arena.

The morning after we arrived, we were welcomed by Bishop Paul N. Sayyah of the Middle East Council of Churches (MECC). Paul, as we came to know him, was the kindest, most thoughtful of bishops. He had made careful plans for our visit and smoothed our path to the doors of interesting and influential people. Paul is also Archbishop of Haifa and the Holy Land, Vicar General of Jerusalem and the Lands under Palestinian Rule, and the Hashemite Kingdom of Jordan. As an Associate General Secretary of MECC, he is deeply involved in ecumenical and inter-faith matters. He had recently returned from Jerusalem where he had been invited to lead the meditations for the pre-Lambeth Conference meeting of Anglican primates. The Anglicans among us felt this indicated a significant ecumenical gesture one we greatly welcomed.

From Paul's introductory talk, we learned something of the religious and political situation, the effect of the war of 1975 to 1992, and we also learned that Christians and Muslims have lived together in harmony in Lebanon for centuries. Indeed, they still do so today in many places, although there are some villages and parts of Beirut where relations are strained.

It soon became clear that to travel anywhere we needed to traverse the busy traffic of Beirut. Despite some road improvements, this was an ordeal. There were no traffic lights or traffic management other than police at junctions in the rush-hour. Rules of the roads were not evident. At least one in our party was continually holding her breath and clutching the seat in front. That we saw no more than the remains of four accidents was amazing!

Once out of the city en route for Byblos, the magnificent mountain scenery impressed us although the more mundane features of our journey were evident in the road checks. There are forty thousand Syrian troops in the country and the road checks are manned jointly with Lebanese soldiers on either side of the road. As we were waved through, the soldier's comment was interpreted for us "God be with you!". We were told that this is a normal greeting; not one we could ever hope to hear, in such circumstances, in England.

Byblos has a charming harbour and extensive ruins. Here, as at other ancient sites, there was none of the careful restoration we have come to expect in the UK One felt it a pity that lack of money probably prevents more being done to preserve the ruins and to guard against the unwary slipping over the edge.

That afternoon we saw the beautiful Kadish valley and visited the Shrine of St Charbel at Bkaa Kafra, as well as a new church with spectacular stained glass high up beneath the roof-line of the sanctuary. The season was Easter, and here it was demonstrated by a model of the empty tomb.

At 7.30 am the next day, we were to discover a new spiritual dimension at the celebration of the mass in the private chapel of the Retreat House where we were staying. The quiet, prayerful setting of the Maronite Liturgy in Arabic, with the prayer of Consecration in Aramaic, the language of Christ's day, seemed so very appropriate. An English translation was provided which enabled us to appreciate the finer points of the liturgy, some of which could be aligned with the Anglican ASB.

The chanting of the Sisters, an integral part of the service, was greatly enjoyed by us all, as was the universal gesture of exchanging the greeting of peace. The liturgy indicated the celebrant saying: "O Lord, may your peace, true love, your eternal and divine graces be with us and among us until the end of the world, and all the days of our lives, and we will offer glory and thanksgiving to you now, and for ever."

That afternoon, we visited Deir-el-Qamar, a village where there had been a 40 day siege of Christians during the war. It was here that Hala, the Bishop's secretary, who had been seconded to us for the duration of our stay, asked if she might hop off the bus to visit the home of her aunt. Within minutes, we were all installed in this home, packed like sardines in the comfortable seating around the walls of a tunnel-shaped room, evidently carved out of the hillside. Uncle and his daughter served us with coffee, Lebanese style, and mamoon, delicious Easter cakes made by each family to an ancient recipe.

We discovered that uncle sang in the local church choir. He sang for us one of the Easter hymns. We responded with "Jesus Christ is risen today" which aroused Aunt from her siesta so that we were able to photograph all family. This was the first of our visit to Christian homes. Next, we went to meet Hala's mother and brother in their Beirut flat, six floors up. This family had evacuated to Beirut from a village during the war. Hala said that she goes back to the village to visit, but cannot stay overnight. It is too frightening. Where they live now is near to a road that was a boundary between opposing forces. There are still some blocks of flats which remain ripped apart. Both Hala's immediate family, and that of her aunt and uncle, lost a daughter in the conflict.

There was what can only be described as an underlying optimism amongst all those we met. The hospitality they offered was more than convention required. One felt that the Christian basis of their lives enabled them to rise above all the uncertainties that still surround them. They had much to give.

We visited the monastery of St Antoinne in the Kadisha valley in glorious sunshine. A chapel hewn out of the rock has the shackles of the saint suspended from an icon above the altar. At some time in the past, a cure for mental illness involved locking the afflicted person in the leg irons, overnight. Some were cured, and some were not so we were told. From there, winding our way upwards on a narrow mountain road, we passed grim reminders of war in the shape of abandoned pill-boxes destined, one felt, to be semi-permanent memorials like similar blots on the landscape in Britain. Here, despite the sunshine, snow covered the mountains. Skiers could be seen in the distance.

Another day we visited the Beqa'a Valley, described in the Bible as the valley of Lebanon. In Roman times, it was exceptionally fertile but seems never quite to have returned to that state of cultivation. The object of this visit was to explore the Roman site Baalbek, an extensive area with remains of enormous structures. The rain put an end to our explorations and we ended up, chilly and wet, in a cafe, where we ate freshly-cooked *lahm bi ajin.* This appeared to be minced lamb and some vegetable on a pizza-like base. Back at the Retreat House, Paul was concerned to hear of this experiment with roadside food. But we all survived without mishap and added this to the list of what became known as our EXPERIENCES.

We were becoming aware, by that time, of how well the group had 'jelled'. We gradually realised what a tremendous blessing this was for an otherwise disparate group of people. There was much fun and laughter. For those of us used to functioning in more formal groups, it was refreshing to be able to be ourselves without the usual inhibitions imposed by role. Reflection on the situation suggests that the whole atmosphere of the retreat house contributed much to this. We experienced very real Christian caring from Bishop Paul and Sisters which led, in a natural way, to responses from us. The fellowship of the Holy Spirit was a reality. For those we met, we had something to offer as a group, as well as individually. A visit to St. Luke's (Anglican) Centre for mentally-handicapped students was one of the highlights of our stay. There are 85 students, of whom 75 are weekly boarders. Teachers work two shifts to cover 24 hours. Funding is being sought to build a new centre. A scheme for Friends of the Centre is being started.

A whole day was spent going south to Sidon and Tyre, both impressive ancient sites where we would have enjoyed lingering longer, had the weather been less unpredictable. The coast road south is of historic importance. From many hundreds of years BC, there is evidence of the land and sea routs on this coast. St Paul himself, on his last journey to Rome put in at Sidon and was cared for by his friends there(Acts27:3). Our travels that day ended at the home of Bishop Paul, in a village where many of his relatives also live. There was much pleasure for us to be entertained there, and to add this dimension to our knowledge of his way of life. He travels a great deal, so the home base is important. On our last evening, there was a service of Thanksgiving in the Chapel of the Retreat House, at which one of our group, Tim Scott, presided. All of us participated in various ways.

Peace does not sit easily in the Lebanon. Much progress has been made but Christians there need our constant prayers, not only for their political situation but also for the work of the Middle East Council of Churches. This particular group may not come together again, but many of us would like to return and we hope that others will follow in our steps. "Peace be with you" now has a very special meaning. "The peace which passes all understanding" was symbolised for us at the final service when Bishop Paul and the Sisters joined us in prayer and thanksgiving.

A Visit to Papua New Guinea.
A small entry in the group diary.

On Saturday 30th May, we went to Kausada to visit the retired Archbishop, Sir George Ambo, a very saintly man, and when we reached his attractive house on the coast he and his wife, Marcella, gave us an ample morning tea with home-made scones. Then Neville drove the four-wheel drive truck in which we travelled along the shore line, carefully gauging the depth of streams that carved channels to the sea in the sand before plunging across as we held our breath. As we drove we waved excitedly to people setting out in dug out canoes with nets on the outrigger platform ready for fishing. We overshot the track to Gona village but turned back and came to the old mission cross still riddled with bullets from when the Japanese began their invasion of Papua New Guinea there.

We were impressed by the very good condition of Gona health centre and the high morale of its staff. After the drive back through the oil palm plantations to Newton college, we had time for a short break before walking down to Joint village to keep our next engagement, an invitation to a cup of tea with Chris and Nancy's village friends, Laban and Ann Hilda. As we walked along the road we heard the empty gas cylinder that served as a village bell ringing out and by the time we reached the village, about half the village were there to welcome us, and by the time we reached the rest-shelter towards which we were guided, the other half had come. Well over a hundred people lined up and we shook the hands of each of them in turn before clambering up the ladder into the rest shelter. There under the palm thatch we were serenaded by the village Sunday School taught by Molly and Phillipa (Nancy and Chris' friend who used to help them with housework) with action songs sung in pidgin English and Orokaivan: the verve of their singing and movement was exhilarating, particularly "Donda tapa baba ga nau ino no ra" (Orokaivan for Lord, all things are yours).

As the singing came to a climax there was another bell and women from the village came bearing plates of home-grown, home-cooked vegetables, mainly root crops such as taro, sweet potato and yam and these were set among us as we sat on the mats in the rest-shelter (note, no tables or chairs). We had a real feast and talked with the village people by a pressure lamp as the night grew on. We learned that Jonah, Lanban's brother, needed a bicycle for his work in the disease prevention unit attached to the hospital, and that gave us something to think about. Finally time came for us to leave and this time we lined up and the hundred or so people filed past to shake our hands before we were driven back the short distance to Newton College in Blasius' minibus. As Janet and John said, "We were so thrilled and moved by everyone's genuine friendship".

Families in Papua New Guinea

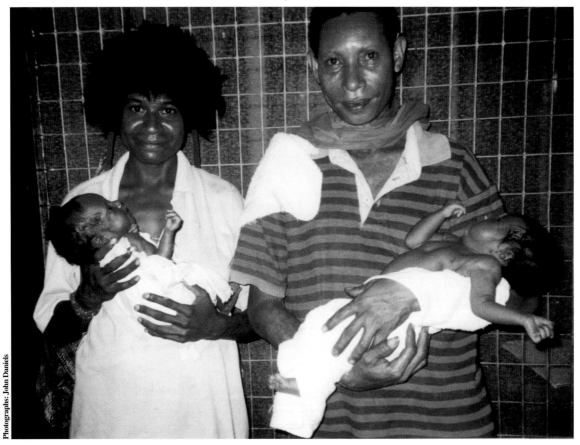

A Visit to Khayelitsha, Cape Town.
Ailsa Moore

Khayelitsha (the word means "New Home" in Xhosa) was founded in 1986. Its creation was controversial. At the time it was built, it was used as a means of excluding certain selected people from the city centre, it was racist. People need work in order to survive, this often means travelling into town and as there is no welfare system, they need to be living near the town. The destruction in the mid 70s of Crossroads the squatter camp, shocked people the world over, but the needs of millions of people were not addressed then and are still not addressed now.

Khayelitsha covers a large area of very sandy Cape Flats, houses need constant sweeping to clear the fine sand from the floors. There are probably around a million people living in the town. The standard of properties varies; some have few facilities, perhaps electric light but no water. Many of the houses are little more than tiny tin huts crowded together, some looked to be without furniture, others are more spacious and well furnished. Every residence is home to some family, I noticed the amount of care taken to keep the houses clean and tidy, there was pride in presenting home as a clean comfortable place.

Khayelitsha has a spirit all of its own. I found in myself a conflict of emotions - admiration at the way the people cope on the one hand and sadness that they are left in such poor conditions on the other. As we drove around the township I felt embarrassment at the thought of being a tourist who had come to gawp at the sight of deprivation from the comfort of a bus. The need to get off the bus and meet some people was very strong. We did visit two bed and breakfast places but these seemed out of place somehow. Who would stay there? They were very comfortable looking. Were they for tourists coming for "the experience" or were they an attempt on behalf of the local people to be more like "the rest of the world". We congratulated the men running these B&Bs on the standard of provision. Perhaps backpackers would want to stay there and experience Khayelitsha; there were some buses running into Cape Town.

One strong lesson that comes from a place like Khayelitcha is how well people make the best out of what they have; they just get on with their lives. I was very impressed by the people we met when we stayed a night in one of the houses. We were made really comfortable, the beds looked lovely. There was no water in the house yet we were given hot water to wash with. The only toilets were outside and had no lights, we were escorted there and warned not to leave the house after dark and we were left buckets to use if needed. It was made clear to us that it was dangerous for us to venture out without an escort because we were not known; this situation has not changed over the years. Inside I felt safe. In the morning we were offered a good breakfast. It appeared that the family had not expected to have three ladies coming to stay and I felt there was some concern about providing us with enough comfort. It was only a pity that there was no time the next day to talk with our hosts and share thoughts and interests. We didn't have time to explain ourselves.

Many of the people living in Khayelitsha need to have some small business to help with earning an income. The family we stayed with cooked some cakes or other tasty items in the evening and people came to buy them. Life must be quite hard though I expect the people of Khayelitsha have become used to this. At the church the next day everyone had come out looking so smart and they put their heart and soul into the worship, the children playing outside were happy and friendly.

On our visits to Khayelitsha we had been entertained by singing, a band playing, children performing, excellent food and wonderful handicrafts to admire and buy.

There is a message to be learnt from the people of this town, I have tried to analyse what it says to me. Coming from such a different background as I do it is really impossible to see things from the point of view of the local people, folk often say, I know how you feel, one never does know how someone else feels. Do any of us really appreciate what it means to belong to the privileged few, the few that have enough, more than enough? If the people of Khayelitsha have reminded me of this and they have, then I must thank them, I was really happy to be their guest. I only wish I could have spent a little longer there and tried to see things through their eyes.

A little Miracle

This is an extract from a book by Philip Marsden, "The Spirit Wrestlers, A Russian Journey," published by Harper Collins. See the reference section for further information about this book.

It was Sunday morning. The road out of Primorsko-Akhtarsk pushed south across a broad tableland of semi-reclaimed marsh. Drainage channels bordered the road and the water was hidden by beds of stooping reeds. The road was very straight but for the odd switch that sent it bucking over a wooded bridge, only to straighten out again on the opposite bank. In the distance the sky was paler blue above the sea. A woman in the hotel had put me onto her brother who was going fishing in the liman. He knew where to find the Old Believers. "Them bearded fellows?" "Course I know them."

His mother had always said that her family had been Old Believers. But he only remembered his grandfather as a Cossack who wore his uniform on saints' days and never went outside in it. "But that's all gone now, all destroyed!"

And now he was going fishing and worried only about the warden, who was armed, and his fellow poachers, who were also armed. "I have only an old pistol and they have kalashnikovs. What can I do? Last week they came in a boat and shot two fishermen."

We reached the Old Believer village of Pokrovka and I waved him off towards the marshes. In the road was a herd of unattended cows, looking this way and that. Beyond them stood a large and newly built church of yellow bricks. Women were spilling out of it in floral head-scarves and nineteenth century dress. Skirting round the cows I went to wait outside for the priest.

Father Gyorgi was a remarkable man. He had a greatness of those blessed with perfect historical timing. His ordination had coincided with the period of the reforms, and he sensed the revived energies of the Pokrovka Old Believers bubbling up around him. He it was who had re-instated the services and re-taught the chants and who, without money, permission or expertise of any kind, had galvanized the community into building themselves a church. And this was no ordinary church. Lacking only in a cupola or two it was a fabulously ambitious structure that would have looked ornate even in a large town. Opposite it stood an open-sided lean-to. There I sat out the heat of the afternoon with Father Gyorgi and a collection of the Pokrovka Old Believers. We arranged ourselves on benches at a long table and drank tea, while a mumble of bantams pecked in the dust. Beyond the flat fields was a line of reeds and beyond them was the sea.

Father Gyorgi wore a rimless cap of burgundy velvet. Shoulder length hair fanned out beneath it. Quietly he invited each of the others to tell their stories or explain to me this point or that. Sometimes he himself would explain and sometimes, when others were talking, I would catch him looking away from us, one hand idly fingering his beard, his placid gaze fixed far off into the marshes.

Another little miracle

128

Wealth

Kim Horner

Returning to Kathmandu to work in a school with children from poor Nepalese families and Tibetan refugees was a way for me to give something back to a place that I'd come to love. I'd spent some weeks traveling around Nepal, taking in the beauty of the mountains and the jungles the previous year, and, eager to return, had discovered a school that required a teacher's services for the Summer.

I was struck by the warm welcome I received from the children, their open, smiling faces which registered happiness. This became all the more amazing as I discovered how they had come to be at the school and saw the basic living conditions they endured. Twenty children slept in a room with 10 bunk begs touching each other, each child's possessions carefully arranged at the end of each bed. The floors and walls were bare concrete. Warm showers were a treat which the younger children had once a week although the warm water often ran out. They told me how lucky they felt. They appeared to have so little, yet they smiled.

I found the children's appreciation of their education amazing, particularly the older ones who spoke about wanting to give back to their society. These students talked of becoming nurses, engineers and teachers to make life better for those less fortunate around them. They felt so fortunate themselves and were inspired to train to have jobs that would make a difference for their families and their people.

At night as I lay in bed reading and reflecting on my day, I would often hear low whispers outside on the balcony. The older students would sit under my window, studying, making use of every ray of low grade electric light that struggled through the thin curtains. An opportunity to do well in the examinations was not to be missed.

From my room I ruminated on the material grasping of the so-called 'developed world' and felt more than content with the few favoured possessions I'd brought with me. I vowed to try, on my return home, to live more simply and be more appreciative of the opportunities I had. I had come here to teach. I was returning home having learnt many valuable lessons.

Home Again

Chapter Five

Home Again

'A man travels the world to find what he needs and returns home to find it.'
George Moore.

Reflecting on your Experiences

For individuals, couples or families returning home there will be plenty to talk over, the experiences of the period of travel, however short, can last for many months, if not years, afterwards. Bringing back a small memento, gifts for friends, photographs and so on can bring lasting fun, but select your memories with care, you want to encourage others not bore them.

A visit or exchange should never be held in a vacuum, but should be the beginning of an on-going friendship. People who travel in groups have often found great value in a re-union after an overseas visit, to share photographs, souvenirs and news, to produce a magazine of the visit, and to decide how to keep in touch with the hosts. It is useful at this stage to share news of books on the area visited, and also to catch up on news of the people and the issues they are facing. Many people do more reading and research after a visit than they do before it, because everything is so much more alive for them after their experiences. Sometimes a group may need to plan the return visit of the host group to their country. The return hospitality of those who have been on an overseas visit is a wonderful contribution to the creativity of the friendship.

It is very helpful for both individual travellers and groups to prepare a presentation of their experiences for their local school, college, place of work, community or church. It is a good idea to collect photographs and slides together before presentations, and to prepare an exhibition of the visit. A magazine of a visit may also be useful, partly as a memento, but also for others to see, and for the use of people who may travel in the same direction in the future.

Sometimes individuals or groups may decide to form an on-going working group following a visit to another country. This might of course include people from the country who live in the home area of the group which has travelled. The development of such a group is simply one way of ensuring that a visit has not been made in a vacuum, and that it will be part of our on-going life and work. This can be particularly helpful to children as it can widen their knowledge and give confidence when they discover how much they have learnt from their travels and what an important contribution they can make to building relationships in their own community.

Living in a New Way

Travelling overseas may leave visitors feeling excited, saddened, uplifted, amazed, changed. After a holiday there is often the anticlimax of getting back to 'normal'. The travels fade from view and life continues much as before. BUT, perhaps we return a slightly different person, having memories of happy encounters and a feeling that we don't want to lose touch with what we found. We may want to keep the links with people we met and with those we travelled with. This can be done through invitations to our homes for our hosts or on-going group meetings with our travelling companions. We may also wish to provide some practical help to people and communities in the country we visited; perhaps to individuals; a handicapped child; a whole community or an oppressed group. We may even feel able to help with schooling for children in an area, or support for the school itself. If we do wish to help in this way then it is vital that we act quickly before the feeling fades. Our involvement and on-going partnership may continue our links for a long time into the future in a very natural way. There is an example of such a friendship in the 'Travellers Tales' section of this book. You may also find the reference section useful if you want to take some action and Christians Aware will also give general advice. For more ideas on what you can do read on.

What you Can do

When you return home feeling full of the excitement of your travel experiences you may find it useful to have some ideas about how it is possible to provide friendship, help and support to some of the people and communities you were in contact with. Here are some thoughts and suggestions that may help.

Donations

One of the easiest ways to donate to a cause of your choice is to support a charity working in the country you have visited. If you find when you get there that there seems to be a need to help children, the elderly, handicapped people, environmental projects or anything else, then you can be fairly sure that there will be a charity working in that field either at home here or in the country itself. Do some research first, get your children involved if necessary, use our reference section, then write to the charity you think may be able to help you and ask for information. Be clear if you want to make a one-off donation or if you want to continue support. Children often want to help animals, please study this area carefully before making a decision. Our government offers extra finance to charities through Gift Aid, you can make your donation larger if you pay tax. The charity will advise you on this. Check to see if the charity is registered, this can be done through the Charities Aid Foundation (CAF) the address is in the reference section at the end of the book.

Sponsorship

Children's education can be sponsored. This may be an excellent way of contributing long-term to the welfare of families. In many cases parents have had little or no chance of obtaining education themselves, if the children can get some schooling then they can contribute in a really positive way to the welfare of the whole family. But remember, sponsorship of this kind needs to be for a long enough time to see the child through education and training. School fees in some parts of the world are very low, but if you can't afford to sponsor a child on your own, you can get joint sponsorship through the agency or charity you choose. Sadly, however, people may begin sponsorship then fail to keep up the payments, real disappointment results. Only consider this long-term commitment if you really want to do it. There are a number of charities running these schemes, refer to the reference section for addresses. An important question to ask is whether the aim is that all the children in an area or school are sponsored or not. If only a few children are sponsored then you may be adding to existing divisions by sponsoring a child. If all the children are to be sponsored then your contribution will be helpful to the whole region, and is not likely to create divisions. It can be possible to make a payment direct to a school but this can be difficult when it comes to the exchange of currency unless you are actually in the country at the time. You will find schools in need of support all over Africa, South America, Asia and many smaller countries.

Adopting an animal

This can be an interesting and exciting project for children. An organisation such as WWF has a number of schemes, again it really means a longer term project though one-off donations are very welcome. In parts of the world where the environment is under threat animals are suffering and many are threatened with extinction. A wonderful way to contribute to the improvement of the planet is to help one of the wild life organisations. When you are buying goods in any country check that animal parts are not used in the production of the item, causing suffering and unnecessary death of the animal.

134

Adopting a granny

Perhaps your travels took you to parts of the world where you came across elderly people in need of help. It is generally easier to get support for children and animals, but harder to find support for the elderly folk. Help the Aged runs schemes for the adoption of elderly, very often homeless and lonely people. They have schemes in Sri Lanka, India, Indonesia, Tanzania, Ethiopia, Cambodia and other countries. The Tibetan elderly also need help and support, those living in Nepal can be assisted through the organisation Help Tibet.

The environment

There is no doubt that travellers come across many issues relating to the environment, the resources of the planet are under great stress and many animal and plant species are facing extinction. The very nature of our planet is being changed and much of this is due to tourism and careless management. In many cases management only recognises three aspects; operators, local people and tourists. The environment supporting these is sometimes almost completely ignored. If human needs are considered to the exclusion of all else, then we face serious erosion of a finite resource. With all this in mind and having returned from your travels, please put some thought into what you observed and consider how you may be able to contribute towards creating a more sustainable environment. Many organisations have set about the task of working tirelessly towards this goal. World Wide Fund for Nature, Earthwatch, Wildlife Conservation Society, Greenforce and many others are tackling some of the problems. Greenpeace and Friend's Of The Earth are well known for their high profile activities. If you feel you really want to help with conservation work then contact one of the organisations for advice. If we really want to continue the most wonderful human experience of being close to nature, then understanding and involvement is needed from everyone.

Human welfare

It is easy for tourists to become so involved with their own enjoyment that they often don't see the real situation for the local population in the country they are visiting. Rarely do tourists see behind the scenes, if they did, they may be shocked by what they find. We hope we have already encouraged you to travel with greater awareness and perhaps you will become interested in the welfare of the local communities where you are staying. Human rights abuses go on in many parts of the world, often un-noticed by the traveller. It is not really wise to get involved in situations where you feel abuses are taking place, keep them in mind, and on your return home, seek advice from an organisation that may be able to advise you.

Amnesty International covers the globe and other organisations may specialise in particular countries. You will find some references at the end of the book.

Fair Trade

Are the goods you buy made through slave trade or fair trade? It is not always easy to know the answer. Ethical trade attempts to encourage companies to improve employment conditions at every stage in the supply chain for products destined for the Western market. To find out which companies are participating in ethical trade, visit www.etl.org,www.fairlab.org, www.cepaa.org

The Traidcraft brand is the guarantee of fair trade, look for it on goods. Traidcraft is listed in the reference section at the end of the book.

A Little Reminder

It is all too easy on arrival home to forget the promise you made to 'write as soon as I get home'! The excitement of the home-coming, telling of the stories, getting back to work or children ready for return to school become the new priorities. Try to set aside some time to write the letter or card and send the photos. Your new friends overseas will be thrilled to know they have not been forgotten. Even if these contacts eventually end, happy memories remain and contribute to a greater sense of well-being.

Some More Reminders

It is so important that pleasure seeking does not blind travellers to issues of immense significance. We include here a few awareness pointers.

Ethics and Tourism

Now that you are back home and can begin to reflect on your travel experiences you may find it useful and interesting to consider some of the implications of tourism in relation to what can be sustainable and what may be purely exploitation. It is usually the non-human members of the planet that are hardest hit by tourism, the sighting of a pride of lions in a safari park can result in forty or fifty land rovers packed with tourists converging on the animals, it reminds one of sightseers at an accident on our roads. There is something really distasteful about this. Man has the responsibility to protect and respect all life on this planet including himself.

Preservation, conservation and exploitation can be measured by the amount of intervention taking place in an environment. In the first situation there is no intervention and the place is left in its natural state. In the second, there is limited intervention designed to create a balance, in the third situation however, there is no limit to the intervention and man develops the area entirely to his own advantage.

On your travels you may have seen conditions that illustrate all three of these situations. Unfortunately exploitation exists where profit becomes the over-riding motivation resulting in the destruction of sustainability. It does appear, however, that public concern is beginning to have an effect and pressure not only from the conservation giants such as Greenpeace but also from the travelling public, is increasingly causing profiteers to reconsider their methods.

The tourist industry still has a long way to go before it can be said to apply codes of ethics which generally are talked of but not put into action. Pressure from the tourist is the most effective way of changing this. All travellers and tourists have a responsibility to conserve and protect the planet, we can all find a way of doing this, however small the contribution it will take us forward to creating a more sustainable future for all life.

If you want to read more about the ethics of tourism there are many books on this subject. One of the best is 'Ecotourism' by David Fennell. Generally these books are available at most libraries.

Your home environment can offer you local actions you can take. Following the Rio Summit of ten years ago on the global environment many local authorities in Britain set up their own Local Agendas for the 21st Century, ie. LA21s. The key to this work is **"Think Globally, Act Locally."** It is well worthwhile checking with your local council to see what is happening to your LA21 agenda, you are likely to find more help is needed for local actions. It is just as important for people to become involved in improving their local environment as it is to assist other parts of the world. Education, recycling, green energy, conservation and so on are all ways in which local people can help the planet to become more sustainable. **Become involved.**

Some Practical Information

Kayapo Chief Kanhoc

Chapter Six

Some Practical Information

Some Books about Travelling

SHADOWS AND WIND. A VIEW OF MODERN VIETNAM
Robert Templer. Little, Brown & Co. 1998
An excellent view of Vietnamese society and some of the problems facing Vietnam today. A very good guide for anyone wishing to visit Vietnam, one of the most beautiful countries in the world.

THE SNOW LEOPARD
Peter Matthiessen. Vintage. 1998
The story of a journey to Crystal Mountain in The Himalayas. A book with a spiritual dimension and a personal story.

ISRAEL, A HISTORY
Martin Gilbert. Doubleday. 1998
A remarkable book written by a man who knows the country intimately. This book will give any traveller to Israel an insight into the turbulent history of a relatively small country.

UNDER THE DRAGON
Rory Maclean. Harper Collins 1998
For anyone thinking of travelling to Burma or anyone wishing to know about this wonderful country, this is the book to read. Sensitive, powerful, honest, compassionate, a journey into a "Betrayed Land".

THE SPIRIT-WRESTLERS A Russian Journey.
Philip Marsden. Harper Collins. 1998
Philip Marsden travels to places unseen for many years, he meets people of enormous courage and gains from them an insight into their way of life revealing the wonders of the human spirit and its passion for survival.

AN UNEXPECTED LIGHT Travels in Afghanistan
Jason Elliot. Picador 1999
Jason Elliot reveals a country greatly hurt by war but one of enormous courage. He faces danger, excitement, beauty and above all the hospitality of people who often had little to give. A remarkable, moving book about a country little seen yet full of wisdom and courage. This book gives an insight into the experience of travel itself.

DO THEY HEAR YOU WHEN YOU CRY
Fauziya Kassindja. Bantam Press 1998
A travel book with a difference. Fauziya Kassindja searches for a country that will provide her with asylum and protection from a forced marriage and the threat of genital mutilation. She travels from Togo via Germany to the USA, there she was shackled, imprisoned and humiliated for sixteen months before, with the help of a young law student, she was granted asylum. A book of great courage and one that causes concern over issues of human rights.

TOUCH THE EARTH
Compiled by T.C.McLuhan. Abacus. 1994

A self-portrait of Indian Existence. This book is a selection of statements and writings of North American Indians. It shows many of the values of Indian Life and causes one to ponder on the way we treat our planet and some of the people who live on it and tend it so lovingly.

BOUND IN MISERY AND IRON
Dave Treece. Survival International 1987

A report on the impact of the Grande Carajas programme on the Indians in Brasil.

BETWEEN EXTREMES
Brian Keenan & John McCarthy. Bantam Press. 1999

Five years after being incarcerated in Lebanon these two men journeyed together this time according to their own rules. They travelled from the north of Chile to Tierra del Fuego. A book describing another type of journey, a journey of friendship and freedom.

THE AGE OF KALI
William Dalrymple. Harper Collins 1998

For those wishing to know and understand more about India than the ordinary traveller would ever discover even from many visits, this book will excite, amaze, horrify yet provide the thrill of discovery of something truly intriguing.

ONE FOOT IN LAOS
Dervla Murphy. John Murray 1999

For the lone traveller this book illustrates both the advantages and disadvantages of travelling alone. Close encounters with almost every problem one can meet with are common place to Dervla Murphy. How she deals with them will provide the reader with food for thought but also good advice.

DAUGHTER OF TIBET
Richen Dolma Taring. Wisdom Publications 1986

A unique autobiography of the life of a Tibetan family living in Tibet before the Chinese occupation. Richen Dolma Taring (Mary) tells of her flight to India and her experiences as an exile.

NO FULL STOPS IN INDIA
Mark Tully. Penguin Books 1992

India is an amazingly maddening yet wonderful country. Mark Tully in a series of ten chapters has written with remarkable insight; a sympathetic, revealing, extraordinary book. It shows a great love of India.

SORROW MOUNTAIN
Ani Pachen and Adelaide Donnelley. Bantam Books 2000

Almost beyond belief, this book is a story of enormous courage. It is the spiritual journey of a Tibetan woman who becomes caught up in the struggle for freedom from the Chinese invasion of Tibet. She survives torture and imprisonment for 21 years eventually escaping over the Himalayas to India where she met the person who inspired her throughout, His Holiness The Dalai Lama.

LOSING CONTROL
Paul Rogers. Pluto Press 2000
This book covers a wide range of issues of enormous importance. Business tourism and the widening gap between rich and poor are but two of the many subjects covered. For everyone interested in the future of our planet, this is essential reading.

TIGERS IN THE SNOW
Peter Matthiessen. Harvill Press 2000
The author expresses, in his own special way, the struggles to protect the future of the Siberian Tiger. A book for nature lovers containing brilliant photographs by Maurice Hornocker and a deep insight into the natural world of these great cats.

WORLD TRAVELLERS ATLAS
Philip's in association with The Royal Geographical Society. 2001
A useful reference book for places of interest and excellent maps covering the globe.

IN SIBERIA
Colin Thubron. Penguin Books 1999
This book has been called a ''masterpiece''. It is an insight into the soul of Siberia. A truly moving book.

TOUCHING MY FATHER'S SOUL
Jamling Tenzing Norgay.   Ebury Press 2001
The author, son of Tenzing Norgay the Sherpa who accompanied Sir Edmund Hillary to the summit of Everest, takes his own journey into the soul of the Everest magic. His desire to come closer to his Father, took him to the summit in 1996 despite enormous problems of avalanches, sickness and fatigue. A compelling book.

THE UKIMWI ROAD
Dervla Murphy. Flamingo 1994
Cycling for three thousand miles from Kenya through Uganda, Tanzania, Malawi and Zambia to Zimbabwe, Dervla Murphy tells a very personal story. The keeping of her sense of humour despite enormous difficulties and her ability to find the best way to communicate with the local people and get their trust, see her through this remarkable journey.

FATU-HIVA. BACK TO NATURE
Thor Heyerdahl. George Allen and Unwin 1974
A real adventure story of a remarkable journey to the island of Fatu-Hiva. A thoughtful book questioning the way man is cutting himself off from nature but finding life in the raw very tough.

FACING THE CONGO
Jeffrey Taylor. Little Brown & Company 2001
Searching for some direction in his life, Jeffrey Taylor takes on a seemingly impossible journey. The might of this African river is to test those who venture on it to the limits. The struggle for survival for those who live on the edges of this great river is described by Taylor with sensitivity and clarity. The flow of the river, and the hustle of life around it,makes this book difficult to put down.

ARABIAN SANDS
Wilfred Thesiger. Harper Collins 2000
This book is about travel among the Arabs undertaken in five years leading up to 1950. It is a book of exploration, encounter and history. There are some brilliant photographs illustrating the life as it used to be in Arabia. This is a book of real quality.

IN SPAIN'S SECRET WILDERNESS
Mike Tomkies. Jonathan Cape Ltd 1989
A naturalist a traveller and an adventurer combine to make Mike Tomkies a favourite storyteller. In Spain he found a wealth of exotic wildlife, perhaps the richest variety in Europe. His love of nature shines through all his writings. A book for nature lovers.

SOUTH FROM BARBARY
Justin Marozzi. Harper Collins 2001
A gruelling journey across the Libyan Sahara by camel takes the reader on a fascinating adventure into inhospitable environments with unpredictable companions.

A treat of history, story telling, sensitivity and brilliant linguistic skills makes this book a must for those with a need for more than a mere travelogue.

ANCIENT FUTURES. Learning from Ladakh
Helena Norburg-Hodge. Rider
Ladakh 'Little Tibet' a beautiful desert land in the Western Himalayas has few resources but for over a thousand years has had a thriving culture. Then came 'development' and this has brought tourist pressures, pollution, unemployment and intolerance. But in Ladakh can still be found inspiration for kinder, intimate and sustainable ways of living. This book analyses and inspires. For a traveller with awareness, a visit to Ladakh would give a peep into a gentler, kinder lifestyle.

TO BE A PILGRIM
Barbara Butler and Jo White. Kevin Mayhew, 2002
A comprehensive guide, information, instruction and inspiration for pilgrims

THE SHADOW OF THE SUN
Ryszard Kapuscinski. Allen Lane, the Penguin Press, 1998
Covering a number of countries in Africa, this book, written by a Polish journalist, gives an insight into the main political events in Africa over the past 50 years. A book really written with the reader in mind, bringing out subtleties of culture and attitudes towards life. The book questions, exposes and penetrates into events, it is not just a text of historical facts.

ECOTOURISM. An introduction
David Fennell. Routledge 1999
For those wanting to understand more about tourism and its effects on the planet this book provides a huge amount of information. It covers a wide range of subjects from the nature of tourism to ethics, marketing and management.

CHARITY CHOICE UK
A very useful reference book listing most of the UK charities dealing with a large range of issues. Can be found in most libraries.

WORLDWIDE VOLUNTEERING FOR YOUNG PEOPLE
Listings of volunteering possibilities for young people, eg the GAP year. Can be found in most libraries.

INTERNATIONAL VOLUNTEERING UK DIRECTORY
Louise Whetter and Victoria Pybus. Can be found in most libraries.

THE WORLD GUIDE. MILLENNIUM EDITION
New Internationalist.
Covers most useful information about 217 countries, for example the population, currency, language, size and other statistics of each country. Can be found in most libraries.

THE COMMUNITY TOURISM GUIDE
Mark Mann. Earthscan & Tourism Concern. 2nd Edition, 2002
Brings together the pick of local community based, locally organised holidays, in hundreds of interesting and often beautiful places around the world, with full contact details and a range of further useful information. Each entry promises a uniquely rewarding experience for adventurous travellers concerned about the impact of their visits.

Kit List

This is a check list only. Travellers may find it useful in helping them to decide what to take and what not to take.

Acriflex antiseptic cream (or similar).

Address labels with addresses. Saves taking an address book.

Anthisan antihistamine cream (or similar).

Anti-malaria pills.

Melolin absorbent dressing.

Antiseptic Wipes. Cuts go septic very quickly in the tropics.

Dioralyte (in various flavours) for any stomach or bowel upset. AVOID anti-diarrhoea medicines, whenever possible.

Drink as much as possible. Coca-Cola is beneficial.

Sterile dressing, 'Micropore' (better than elastoplast).

Paracetamol (or similar).

Puritabs / Sterotabs – These make the water taste horrible.

Vitamin C flavoured tablets improve the flavour of the puritabs.

Dramamine to reduce swelling from insect bites.

Optrex for dusty eyes.

Insect Repellent like Jungle Formula. Be careful – it dissolves plastic!

Book. One good one. Swap around in the group while you are travelling, leave it behind when you return home.

Family Photographs.

Map of the area.

Bottle Opener.

Scissors, sewing kit and safety pins.

Pocket knife and spoon.

Camera plus films plus spare battery.

Clothes pegs.

Notebook or diary, ball-point pen and pencil.

Plastic mug and plate.

Plastic bags.

Plugs – universal basin and universal electrical.

Talcum powder – Baby powder is best.

Cotton underwear/socks. Synthetics can cause a rash.

Jersey. It can be quite cold in the early morning or evening.

Long sleeved shirt.

Money belt. Cotton. Plastic bag for currency notes.

Rain-proof top.

Lightweight rucksack. Don't buy one so large that you can't carry it when full. Beware of putting valuables in the outside pockets.

Shoes. Well tried and comfortable (not new!).

Mosquito net.

Sleeping bag. One that fully unzips is best because you may want to sleep on or under it when hot rather than in it! (cotton or silk are good).

Pillow case.

Cotton sleeping sheet.

Water bottle.

String or thin nylon cord.

Sun hat, sun tan/burn cream/lotion and sun glasses.
Head Scarf (Women).
Swim suit and towel plus extra towel.
Tea towels. Have many uses.
Toilet roll.
Torch. Tiny Duracell ones are good.
Cheap watch.
US dollars for emergency money and airport tax.

Vaccinations. Go to your doctor as soon as your visit is planned, details in "Staying Healthy In Africa".
Keep adequate supplies of any necessary medication in two separate places plus Doctor's letter if necessary.

Handy Hints

Empty film containers are useful for pills, creams, etc. Rigid plastic container for tubes of cream etc., to avoid squashing. Pack first aid items in labelled, closed plastic bags.

If you are a real enthusiast or just a fascinated onlooker then Survival Aids offers "the Survival Catalogue for summer travellers, your complete guide to the most comprehensive range of hot weather clothing and equipment available." Their address is:

Survival Aids Limited, Morland, Penrith, Cumbria CA 10 3AZ. Tel: 01931 4444

A-Z on being hosted in homes or guest houses

A 'going with the flow' motto could not be more apt when being hosted. Those of us who have delighted in or have been bemused by households who have welcomed us to stay have stories to tell. However, telling tales can be embarrassing and an abuse of hospitality. Enquiries of travellers who have been hosted in Africa, Asia and Latin America sparked off this A-Z advice which carries no names, and the staccato style is light hearted in intent! Do play the game by trying out lists of your own, before and after a visit! You can improve on this one.

A-C

The attitude of a guest is fundamental, which invariably amounts to the acceptance of what is on offer. Beds may vary and unexpected bugs may be encountered, but contacts are being made with those willing to host strangers. Mission is about contact, concern and compassion. It may be that Christ's commission (Matthew 28.19) will have a place once relationships have been established, but the stay is likely to be more about receiving than giving.

D-F

Dialogue about differences has a place, but an emphasis on disparities can lead to hasty judgements that may later be regretted. Enjoying yourself is the key and empathy is more likely if controlled excitement is maintained throughout the encounter. Embarrassments may occur, but a sense of humour helps overcome them and they can be put into better perspective when evaluating the visit. Friendships of longstanding can result, the more so if there is a follow-up correspondence once home again.

G-H

Greetings and farewells in the local language make a difference and the taking of modest gifts can be evidence of goodwill. Being asked for gifts during or after visits can present problems and advice is best sought from those who understand such requests. A good hug, when culturally acceptable, communicates a common humanity, particularly during the HIV/AIDS pandemic.

I-M

Identifying with each member of a household can provide insights across cultures that distance normally prevents. But, beware of jumping to conclusions particularly about issues of justice about which strong feelings are held. Kids are often an entry point for developing relationships; the language of play and laughter with children can readily link people together. Manners vary from place to place, so be wary, particularly at mealtimes. It helps, for instance, if whatever food is offered is eaten and enjoyed.

N-R

Noises, known and those unidentifiable – during the day or night – can be seen as interesting rather than odd! Being open about what delights or what really disturbs, particularly over matters of privacy, makes for honest relationships. In what is possibly an opportunity of a lifetime, patience and perseverance may be essential. Having photographs with you of your home and family can prove a conversation starter, but talk about politics needs to be treated with care. Questions worth asking often come after there has been time and space for reflection, which can be difficult to find in a busy household and during a packed programme. Requests too may then be made more sensitively.

S-W

Sharing in Sunday worship, when possible, can prove a bonding experience. So too can storytelling, both by the host's family and, sparingly, by the guest! It can also be a source of smiles. Singing and dancing together are even better. Such time given to be with hosts is mutually beneficial. Tummy troubles and toilets can be troublesome and having a torch can be helpful. Interminable television can be as much of a problem as elsewhere.

The understanding visitors will as far as possible vary their programmes to suit the host. In dry areas water will be used economically and in hot ones they will wash with even more care!

X-Z

Xenophobia sufferers (fear of foreigners) should avoid such hosting and remember you are not visiting a zoo.

Guide Notes on the use of information supplied by embassies and national tourist boards

Most embassies provide some form of information for the traveller, which can be sent by post on request. This includes visa and health information, news about currency controls and sometimes items such as motoring regulations, insurance requirements etc. Clearly, some governments, for their own reasons, are much keener to encourage, or discourage, certain kinds of visitors than others. For this reason, care and tact should always be used in approaching official representatives of countries you plan to visit, especially when it is known that the government – or at any rate influential factions within a country, may be indifferent or even hostile to Christianity, even to bodies with aims like those of Christians Aware. When applying for a visa, or when arriving in a country where visas are given on entry, the purpose of your visit should always be stated simply as tourism. If you are asked before travel or on arrival to write on a visa form the name and address of local host contacts make sure that they have 'cleared' your visit and are in good standing with the authorities. It is always a good idea to make contact with the knowledgeable nationals of the countries concerned before you travel: they can tell you some of the things to do or not to do in their country, especially when approaching embassy officials or dealing with officials during your stay. In some cases, discretion may be needed in contacting foreign nationals living in this country before or after your trip: they may be political refugees etc. Some governments are more paranoid than others. Respect and honest shrewdness are the watchword: always follow the 'cues' of nationals (or local hosts) in countries you visit. Never do anything that puts them at risk or makes them embarrassed. Finally, bureaucracy is endemic to the human condition: always be patient! In general, losing one's temper is counter-productive.

National tourist boards may often be or wish to appear to be very friendly and helpful. Either way, remember that they are often in business to sell you the image of their country which they want you to buy, rather than the image which will help you to see the country as it really is. After all, human nature being as it is, none of us is too keen to show all of ourselves as we really are, and there is not too much difference between tourist offices and the best or worst of motives found among the businesses down the average high street or in the 'Yellow Pages'. Again, be alert, respectful, as with embassies, so with national tourist offices, try to find out from relatives, friends, colleagues and/or contacts with nationals something about a country, its outlook and the way it works before contacting the embassy or tourist office. That way, you can find out how they can serve you best.

Web sites

This principle especially holds good when you make your first enquiries about a country by visiting the web sites of its embassy, or high commission, (for all Commonwealth states), or of its national tourist board. Be discerning over what is not said, or shown, as well as what is said or displayed, and over how official information is presented on such web sites. In particular, in the case of states whose governments have controversial stances on human rights, the environment, development issues etc, be very careful about answering apparently innocent, but sometimes cleverly designed on-screen questionnaires, or entering 'holiday competitions' or similar offers. Among these may be intelligence gathering devices dressed up as tourism or business promotion. Completing such on – line enquiries may inadvertently give the web site owners more details than they might properly be entitled to (or certainly more data than you might wish to reveal!) about yourself and/or your motives for visiting the country concerned. At the very least, beware of web sites which seem only too keen to send you either on-line or via 'snail mail' unsolicited information including 'pressure' sales material on the supposed tourist delights, political virtues and business opportunities in the countries concerned. Again, the 'bottom line' here is 'be discerning' whilst also avoiding cynicism over some at least of the motives of certain official and /or commercial travel web site operators!

Specified References

Contact details of each of the following organisations is to be found in the main reference section or in the book section.

Animal Welfare organisations
Butterfly Gardeners Association
Earthwatch Institute
Ecotravellers'
Greenforce
Greenpeace
International Fund For Animal Welfare
World Wide Fund For Nature
WSPA. World Society for the Protection of Animals.

Children's Support and sponsorship
Bible Lands Society
Children of The Andes
Estrela
Railway Children
SOS Children's Villages
Tibet Society

Conservation
BTCV
Butterfly Gardeners Association
Coral Cay
Earthwatch
Ecotravellers
Friends of The Earth
Greenforce
Greenpeace
World Wide Fund For Nature

Human Rights
Amnesty International
Anti-Slavery
Burma Campaign
Free Tibet Campaign
Medical Foundation for Victims of Torture
Survival International

Support for Disadvantaged
Bible Lands
Cafedirect
Help Tibet
Sight Savers
The British Red Cross
Traidcraft
Water Aid
Leprosy Mission

General Information regarding travel
Christians Aware
Ecotravellers
HCPT Pilgrimage Trust
International Volunteering Guide
The Imaginative Traveller – Group Travel
Tourism Concern
Voluntary Service Overseas
Worldwide Opportunities On Organic Farms
Worldwide Volunteering for Young People
Traidcraft run expeditions to India, usually in October, to visit producers.
ACE Study Tours organise cultural tours in the UK and overseas.

Holidays For People With Disabilities
Far Frontiers
Parkinson's Disease Society
Winged Fellowship Trust

General Reference Books or magazines
New Internationalist
Tibet Information Network
Tourism Concern
World Traveller's Atlas.

General Reference Section

Organisations

ACE Study Tours. Babraham, Cambridge. CB2 4AP. Tel 01223 835055 Fax 01223 837394.
e-mail ace@study-tours.org www.study-tours.org
From ACE Study Tours you can obtain a list of various cultural tours covering art, music, architecture, drama, ecology, wildlife and archaeology. Though many of these guided tours are quite expensive, some are not. Find out for yourself. There are some week-end courses run in this country, free brochures are available on request.

Amnesty International UK Section. 99-119 Rosebery Avenue, London, EC1R 4RE.
Tel 020 7417 6385. www.amnesty.org.uk
Amnesty International's mandate is to promote the values of the Universal Declaration of Human Rights, and to work worldwide for the release of prisoners of conscience, fair trials for political prisoners and an end to torture, extra-judicial executions, 'disappearances' and the death penalty.

Anti-Slavery International. Thomas Clarkson House, The Stableyard, Broomgrove Road, London. SW9 9TL. Tel 020 7501 8920. e-mail antislavery@antislavery.org www.antislavery.org
Anti-slavery International is committed to eliminating slavery through research, raising awareness and campaigning. By pressurising governments to acknowledge slavery and abolish its practice, and by giving local organisations an international voice, they increase the power for change. It is inconceivable that as we enter the 21st century, slavery is allowed to exist. They will continue to fight against slavery until everyone is free.

Bible Lands Society. P.O Box 50 High Wycombe. Bucks. HP15 7QU
Tel 01494 897950 Fax 01494 897951. e-mail info@biblelands.co.uk
Bible Lands supports Christian-led schools, vocational training, children's homes, hospitals and rehabilitation centres in the Holy Land, Egypt and Lebanon in the main. Children are from poor and broken families, some have disabilities others are orphans or refugees. All of them suffer from the constant tensions of the region in which they live.

Bird Finders' Holidays for birdwatchers. For details contact Vaughan Ashby, 18, Midleeaze, Sherbourne, Dorset. DT9 6DY. Telephone: 01935 817001. E-mail:Birdfinders@compuserve.co.uk

BTCV 36, St Mary's Street, Wallingford. OX10 0EU. Tel 01491 821660. Fax 01491 839646.
e-mail information@btcv.org.uk www.btcv.org
For finding out about conservation holidays in the UK and abroad.

Burma Campaign UK. Third Floor, Bickerton House, 25-27 Bickerton Road. London. N19 5JT.
Tel 020 7281 7377. Fax 020 7272 3559. e-mail bagp@gn.apc.org www.burmacampaign.org.uk
The Burma Campaign campaigns for human rights and democracy in Burma. They work for all the peoples of Burma regardless of race, ethnicity, gender or age.

Butterfly Gardeners Association, Association and Project Chrysalis. 1563 Solano Avenue, 477 Berkeley CA 94707 . USA. Tel 001 510 5287730.
Project Chrysalis is a therapeutic programme. There are also projects from environmental education, violence prevention to improvement of habitats and parks. See also Travelling Titbits, chapter 3.

Cafedirect. 10a, Queensferry Street, Edinburgh, EH2 4PG. Tel 0345 660192
e-mail info@cafedirect.co.uk www.cafedirect.co.uk
Supporting the growers of tea and coffee.

Charities Aid Foundation. Kings Hill, West Malling, Kent. ME19 4TA. Tel 01732 520001
www.allaboutgiving.org
C.A.F. provides information about various ways of giving to charity and how to make it tax
effective.

Children of The Andes. 301 Kentish Town Road, London NW5 2TJ.
Tel 020 7485 8634. Fax 020 7485 8690. e-mail info@children-of-the-andes.org
www.children-of-the-andes.org
This charity supports Columbian NGOs working to reverse the trend towards violence and
exclusion faced by a growing number of young children in Columbia. It is the children who suffer
most in this country, considered by the UN to be the most dangerous in the world for children. The
projects supported help children to make their own decisions and take control of their futures.
Empowering children in this way involves giving them support, access to resources and the
chance to learn vocational skills. At the same time, the projects work hard to change society's
attitude to their plight. The changes being striven for will not happen overnight; long- term
sustainable projects are needed. The work contributes to aiding the plight of street children at risk
in Columbia

Christians Aware. 2, Saxby Street, Leicester. LE2 0ND. Tel/fax 0116 254 0770
e-mail barbarabutler@christiansaware.co.uk www.christiansaware.co.uk
Christians Aware gives information regarding individual and group travel. It also organises a
number of overseas group visits annually.

Coral Cay Conservation Expeditions. 154 Clapham Park Road,. London. SW4 7DE. Tel 0870
750 0668. e-mail information@coralcay.org www.coralcay.org

Earthwatch Institute. 57 Woodstock Road, Oxford. OX2 6HJ. Tel 01865 318838
Fax 01865 311383. e-mail info@earthwatch.org.uk www.earthwatch.org/europe
Earthwatch promotes sustainable conservation of our natural resources and cultural heritage by
supporting scientific field research and education.

Ecotravellers' Wildlife Guides. Customer Services Department. Harcourt Publishers Ltd. Foots
Cray High Street, Sidcup. Kent. DA14 5HP. Tel 020 8308 5700. Fax 020 8308 5702. e-mail
wildlife@harcourt.com www.harcourt-international.com

Estrela. 19, Powell Street, Hartlepool. TS26 9BN. Tel 0191 2653009. Fax 01429 265379.
This charity aims to develop people to people links between Brasil and Britain to broaden
understanding and achieve social inclusion, primarily through community arts, co-operation and
exchange.
In Brasil, Estrela works alongside Brasilian youth and community initiatives in Sao Paulo and
Salvador and also has connections in Fortaleza and Rio. They offer technical and financial co-
operation to their main partners who are Estrela Nova (community initiative with young people at
risk in Sao Paulo) and Ativacao (youth and community theatre collective in Salvador).

Fairtrade Foundation. Suite 204 16, Baldwin's Gardens. London EC1N 7RJ.
Tel 020 7405 5942. e-mail mail@fairtrade.org.uk www.fairtrade.org.uk
Look for the **Fairtrade** symbol on goods to guarantee a better deal for Third World Producers.

Far Frontiers. info@farfrontiers.com They link with The Parkinson's Disease Society in organising expeditions.

Free Tibet Campaign. 1, Rosoman Place, London. EC1R 0JY. Tel 0207833 3838
e-mail @freetibet.org www.freetibet.org
Free Tibet Campaign stands for the right of Tibetans to determine their own future. It campaigns for an end to the Chinese occupation of Tibet and for the Tibetan's fundamental human rights to be respected. Advice on the advisability of travelling to Tibet may be obtained if required.

Foreign & Commonwealth Office. Offers 24 hour advice at: Travel Advice Unit, Consular Division, Foreign & Commonwealth Office, Old Admiralty Buildings, London SWA 2PA.
Tel: 0870 6060290. e-mail consular.fco@gtnet.gov.uk www.fco.gov.uk

Greenforce. 11, Betterton Street, Covent Garden, London. WC2H 9BP. Tel 020 7470 8888. Fax 020 7470 8889. e-mail GREENFORCE@btinternet.co. www.greenforce.org
Greenforce provides support to safeguard the biodiversity of threatened ecosystems. It runs expeditions and provides other services.

Greenpeace. Canonbury Villas. London. N1 2PN Tel. 020 7685 8100.
e-mail supporter@uk.greenpeace.org www.greenpeace.org.uk

HCPT The Pilgrimage Trust. 100a High Street, Banstead, Surrey. SM7 2RB. Tel 01737 353311 Fax 01737 353008. e-mail hq@hcpt.org.uk www.hcpt.org.uk Arrange pilgrimages to Lourdes.

Help The Aged. St James's Walk, Clerkenwell Green, London. EC1R 0BE. Tel 020 7253 0253. Fax 020 7250 4474. e-mail hta@dial.pipex.com
Help The Aged runs some adoption schemes for elderly people in countries such as: Ethiopia, Thailand, Tanzania, India, Sri Lanka, Indonesia and others.

Help Tibet. P.O.Box 138, Barnes, London. SW13 9RN. Tel/Fax 020 8748 8784
Support for elderly Tibetan people in Nepal.

International Fund For Animal Welfare. P.O.Box 138 Moulton House, Pondwood Close, Northampton. NN3 6WB.
They offer advice and ways of supporting wildlife.

Imaginative Traveller. 14 Barley Mow Passage. Chiswick. London. W4 4PH. Tel 020 8742 8612. Fax 020 8742 3045.
They offer a variety of tours, for individuals or for small groups to various parts of the world. You can also make contact via e-mail sundowners@imtravel.co.uk or look at the web site on www.adventurebound.co.uk

ISEC. The International Society for Ecology and Culture. Foxhole, Dartington, Devon. TQ9 6EB Tel: 01803 868650. Fax: 01803 868651. e-mail: isecuk@gn.apc.org www.isec.org.uk
This is a non-profit organisation concerned with the protection of both biological and cultural diversity. The emphasis is on education for action.

John Grooms. Working With Disabled People. 50 Scrutton Street. London. EC2A 4XQ. Tel 020 7452 2000 Fax 020 7452 2001. e-mail charity@johngrooms.org.uk www.charity.johngrooms.org.uk
Provision of some holiday accommodation overseas for disabled people.

Key Travel. 1st Floor, 28-32 Britannia Street, London. WC1X 9JF. Tel: 020 7843 9600. Fax: 020 7278 8035. e-mail (name)@keytravel.co.uk www.keytravel.co.uk and Queens House, Queen Street, Manchester. M2 5HT Tel: 0161 819 8900. Fax: 0160 839 3893.
Key Travel offers help with complicated itineraries and special advice to churches, Christian travellers and Christian organisations.

Leprosy Mission. Goldhay Way, Orton Goldhay, Petergorough. PE2 5GZ. Tel 01733 370505. Fax 01733 404880. e-mail post@tlmew.org.uk
Founded in 1874 to support a small leper colony in north-west India, the Leprosy Mission now runs a network of hospitals and training centres in the subcontinent, as well as leprosy control and rehabilitation programmes in 30 other developing countries. They care for some 200,000 leprosy patients.

Medical Foundation for Victims of Torture. Star House, 104/108 Grafton Road, London. NW5 3YP. Tel 020 7813 9999. Fax 020 7813 0033. www.torturecare.org.uk

New Internationalist. Tower House, Lathkill Street, Market Harborough. LE16 9EF. Tel 01858 438896. Fax 01858 434958. www.newint.org
New Internationalist exists to report on the issues of world poverty and inequality; to focus attention on the unjust relationship between the powerful and the powerless in both rich and poor nations; to debate and campaign for the radical changes necessary within and between those nations if the basic material and spiritual needs of all are to be met; and to bring to life the people, the ideas, the action in the fight for racial justice. N.I. produces a monthly publication dealing with the above.

North South Travel. For discounts when travelling contact North South Travel, Moulsham Mill, Parkway, Chelmsford, Essex. CM2 7PX. Tel/Fax: 01245 608291

Oxfam. 274 Banbury Road, Oxford OX2 7DZ. Tel 01865 312409. www.oxfam.org.uk
Oxfam provides support for deprived people and communities throughout the world.

Parkinson's Disease Society. 215, Vauxhall Bridge Road, London. SW1V 1EJ. Tel 020 7931 8080.or 020 7932 1347. e.mail expeditions@parkinsons.org.uk
They offer advice for people with Parkinson's Disease wishing to travel and organise expeditions for others in association with Far Frontiers.

Railway Children. Unit G8, Scope House, Weston Road, Crewe, Cheshire. CW1 1DD. Tel/Fax 1270 251571. e-mail railway.children@virgin.net www.railwaychildren.org.uk
This is a charity working on behalf of the children who live in or around the world's railway stations. Its purpose is to work in partnership with existing children's and street children's projects and charities, providing them with money and other help they may need. Two types of help are provided; a point of contact for children coming onto the streets and giving help and advice; providing a shelter as a way of getting them off the streets and into long-term housing. At the refuge the children are offered health care, education, training, advocacy and protection from abuse.

Saga. The mature traveller may find that Saga offers helpful information. Saga has many years of experience of arranging holidays. For more information contact: Saga Holidays Ltd. The Saga Building, Enbrooke Park, Folkstone, Kent. CT20 3SE. www.saga.co.uk

Sight Savers. Grosvenor Hall, Bolnore Road, Haywards Heath. W. Sussex. RH16 4BX. Tel 01444 446600 Fax 01444 446688. e-mail information@sightsaversint.org.uk www.sightsavers.org.uk Sight Savers offers treatment and support for people in the developing world who have visual disabilities.

Shared Interest Society Limited. 25, Collingwood Street, Newcastle upon Tyne. NE1 1JE. Tel: 0191 233 9100. Fax: 0191 233 9110. e-mail: post@shared-interest.com www.shared-interest.co. A cooperative lending society which gives people the opportunity to invest positively in the South to benefit poor people and their communities. Individuals can invest a sum of money to be used as a loan. Interest may be taken or returned into the loan, the investment can eventually be reclaimed. This scheme works alongside fair trade and can ensure that the people making goods in poorer countries can buy the materials needed.

SOS Children's Villages. 32A Bridge Street, Cambridge. CB2 1UJ. Tel 01223 365589 Fax 01223 322613.
The aim of SOS Children's Villages is to give orphaned and abandoned children a mother, a family and a home in a village that is part of a wider community, caring for them until they achieve independence, thus leading to a better future. SOS works in a number of countries around the world. Web site:www.sos-uk.org.uk

Survival International. 6, Charterhouse Buildings. London.EC1M 7ET. Tel 020 7687 8700. Fax 020 7687 8701. e-mail info@survival-international.org www.survival-international.org **Survival International** is a worldwide movement to support tribal peoples. It stands for their right to decide their own future and helps them protect their lands, environment and way of life.

The British Red Cross. 9, Grosvenor Crescent. London. SW1X 7EJ Tel 020 7235 5454. Fax 020 7235 7447 www.redcross.org.uk

Tibetan Environment Network. T.E.N. 10, Dunstable Road, Richmond. TW9 1UH. Tel 020 8940 3166. e-mail dalha@aol.com www.tibetanenvironment.net A non-political, non-governmental and non-profit making self-help organisation set up to assist the Tibetan community and the local community living in Ladakh. They work in the field of the environment, ecology, health and appropriate high altitude farming.

Tibet Society. Unit 9 139, Fonthill Road, London. N4 3HF. Tel 020 7272 1414. Fax 020 7272 1410. e-mail members@tibet-society.org.uk www.tibet-society.org.uk The objects of the Tibet Society are; by non-party political action to promote the cause of Tibetan independence and to bring before the world the sufferings of the oppressed people of Tibet; To assist those Tibetans who fled over the Himalayas to India and elsewhere; To promote understanding of Tibetan history, culture and religion-both on account of the great intrinsic value which such studies have for the west and that we may more effectively befriend the exiled people of Tibet.

Tibet Information Network. City Cloisters, 188-196 Old Street, London. EC1V 9FR Tel 020 7814 9011. Fax 020 7814 9015. e-mail tin@tibetinfo.net www.tibetinfo.net T.I.N. provides an up-to-date information service on the situation in Tibet. They offer a free e-mail service of the above.

Traidcraft. Suite 308, 16, Baldwin's Gardens, London EC1N 7RJ. Tel 020 7242 3955.
Fax 020 7242 6173. e-mail helnm@traidcraft.co.uk www.traidcraft.co.uk
Traidcraft fights poverty through trade.
Also: Traidcraft plc. Kingsway, Gateshead, Tyne and Wear. NE11 0NE.
Tel 0191 491 0591. Fax 0191 482 2690. e-mail sales@traidcraft.co.uk
www.traidcraft.co.uk
At this address you can obtain a catalogue of goods. If you ask for Catharine Howe you will get
details of annual trips to India, usually in October, to visit producers, these are organised trips.

Travel Friends International. This is a consultancy organisation that can help with travel plans.
This is a free service. It offers free advice on countries of your choice taken from their brochure,
quotations on air fares and links with partner organisations in the countries listed. Apply for information
from: Travel Friends International, St. Clare, The Street, Parkenham, Bury St. Edmunds, Suffolk.
IP31 2JU. Tel/Fax: 01 359 232385. e-mail: finchtravelfriends@talk21.com

Travelling Naturalist. Wildlife holidays. For information on a variety of wildlife holidays in many
countries contact: The Travelling Naturalist, PO Box 3141, Dorchester. DT1 2XD. Tel: 01305 267994.
Fax: 01305 265506. e-mail: Jamie@naturalist.co.uk www.naturalist.co.uk

Tourism Concern. Stapleton House, 277-281 Holloway Road, London N7 8HN. Tel 020 7753 3330
Fax 020 7753 3331. e-mail info@tourismconcern.org.uk www.tourismconcern.org.uk
Tourism is the world's largest industry, affecting the lives of millions of people worldwide. But
while tourism development is big business, local people rarely benefit. Tourism is a **fair trade** issue.
People living in many tourist destinations are now counting the cost of development which has
failed to put their interests on a par with those of their visitors. Tourism Concern is an organisation
for people who care about both the quality of experience for the tourist and the quality of life for the
people who live there.

UK Foreign Office

VegiVentures. Castle Cottage, Castle Acres, Norfolk. PE32 2AJ. Tel 01760 755888.
www.vegiventures.com
They offer breaks into other lands and cultures. They offer ventures into Peru, Turkey and other
places. All vegetarian or vegan food.

Voluntary Service Overseas. 137 Putney Bridge Road, London. SW15 2PN. Tel 020 8780 7500.
Fax 020 8780 7207. e-mail enquiry@vso.org.uk www.vso.org.uk
V.S.O. provides some opportunities for working overseas.

Water Aid. Prince Consort House, 27-29 Albert Embankment, London. SE1 7UB
Tel 020 7793 4500. Fax 020 7793 4545. e-mail wateraid@wateraid.org.uk
www.wateraid.org.uk
They provide safe water and sanitation in developing countries for many people who have no
access to these essentials. They also provide some training for local people in the use of
equipment for provision of safe water.

Wildlife Trusts. Marine Appeal. For those interested in saving our seas from pollution and other
problems contact: The Kiln, Waterside, Mather Road, Newark. NG24 1WT
Tel. 01636 677711 Fax 01636 670001 . e-mail marineappeal@wildlife-trusts.cix.co.uk
www.wildlifetrusts.org
Protecting wildlife for the future. They have a particular interest in marine wildlife

Winged Fellowship Trust. Angel House, 20-32 Pentonville Road. London. N1 9XD. Tel 020 7833 2594 Fax 020 7287 0216. e-mail admin@wft.org.uk www.wft.org.uk
Arrange holidays for people with disabilities through New Discovery Holidays Worldwide.

World Society for the Protection of Animals. WSPA. 89, Albert Embankment, London. SE1 7TP. Tel: 0207587 5000 Fax: 020 7793 0208 e-mail: wspa@wspa.org.uk www.wspa.og.uk
Should anyone come across animals being ill-treated in any part of the world this society does take action and it is good to know that WSPA cares. WSPA has consultative status at the United Nations and the Council of Europe.

World Wide Opportunities On Organic Farms. WWOOF. PO Box 2675 Lewes, E. Sussex. BN7 1RB. (S.A.E. please) www.wwoof.org
This is an exchange network whereby accommodation and practical experience are given in return for work on organic farms and smallholdings. No previous experience needed. There are hosts in some 49 countries. There are benefits for host and volunteer alike.

World Wide Fund For Nature. Panda House, Weyside Park, Godalming. Surrey. GU7 1XR. Tel 01483 426444 Fax 01483 726409. www.wwf-uk.org
WWF provides excellent information on travel activities for children. It has produced a number of very helpful books on tourism and wildlife. It runs a number of wildlife sponsorship schemes for endangered animals.

GO IN SEARCH OF

YOUR PEOPLE

LOVE THEM

LEARN FROM THEM

PLAN WITH THEM

SERVE THEM.

BEGIN WITH WHAT THEY KNOW

BUILD ON WHAT THEY HAVE

BUT OF THE BEST LEADERS

WHEN THEIR TASK IS ACCOMPLISHED

THEIR WORK IS DONE

THE PEOPLE WILL SAY

"WE HAVE DONE IT OURSELVES."

"Here we have a guidebook with a difference, a guide to humane, intelligent travelling. While offering much sound advice to the novice, "Go to the People," will also help those who have wearied of conventional tours – perhaps in organized tours, perhaps as back-packers – and wish to experience other lands not merely as onlookers/fun-seekers."

Dervla Murphy in her foreword to "Go to the People. Travel with Awareness."